Preschool English Learners

Principles and Practices to Promote Language, Literacy, and Learning

A Resource Guide

Publishing Information

Preschool English Learners: Principles and Practices to Promote Language, Literacy, and Learning—A Resource Guide was developed by WestEd's Center for Child and Family Studies for the Child Development Division, California Department of Education. It was prepared for printing by the staff of CDE Press under the direction of Sheila Bruton: editing, Edward T. O'Malley; cover and interior design, Cheryl McDonald; typesetting, Jeannette Reyes. It was published by the Department, 1430 N Street, Sacramento, CA 95814-5901. It was distributed under the provisions of the Library Distribution Act and *Government Code* Section 11096.

ISBN 978-0-8011-1667-4

Ordering Information

Copies of this publication are available for $15.95 each, plus shipping and handling charges. California residents are charged sales tax. Orders may be sent to the California Department of Education, CDE Press, Sales Office, 1430 N Street, Suite 3207, Sacramento, CA 95814-5901; FAX (916) 323-0823.

An illustrated *Educational Resources Catalog* describing publications, videos, and other instructional media available from the Department can be obtained without charge by writing to the address given above or by calling the Sales Office at (916) 445-1260.

Notice

The guidance in *Preschool English Learners: Principles and Practices to Promote Language, Literacy, and Learning—A Resource Guide* is not binding on local educational agencies or other entities. Except for the statutes, regulations, and court decisions that are referenced herein, the document is exemplary, and compliance with it is not mandatory. (See *Education Code* Section 33308.5.)

Contents

A Message from the State Superintendent of Public Instruction v

Acknowledgments vi

Chapter One: Introduction to the Resource Guide 1
What You Will Find in This Guide 2
Core Beliefs 3
Principles and Practices: Children as Active Learners 4
Summary of the Guide by Chapter 5
Continued Professional Development.................................... 6

Chapter Two: Preschool English Learners,
Their Families, and Their Communities 9
The Children.. 10
The Role of Families in Language and Literacy
    Development... 13
The Diversity of the Immigration Experience 14
Connecting School and the Home Language...................... 14
Varieties of Language 17

Chapter Three: Connecting First
and Second Languages 19
Children and Their Language Development........................ 20
The Components of Language.. 22
A Wide Range of Language Practices 25
Awareness of How Language Works 29
The Influence of Peers on Language Development............. 30

Chapter Four: Paths to Bilingualism 33
Theoretical Basis for Supporting Bilingualism.................... 34
Simultaneous Bilingualism 36
    Early Phase (Birth to Three Years)................................ 37
    Middle Phase (Three to Four Years) 38
    Later Phase (Five to Six Years)..................................... 39
Successive Bilingualism... 41
Receptive Bilingualism.. 42

Chapter Five: Stages and Strategies in Second-Language Acquisition 45
Stages of Learning a Second Language 46
    The Use of the Home Language to Communicate 47
    The Observational and Listening Period 47
    Telegraphic and Formulaic Speech 48
    Fluid Language Use 50
Strategies in Second-Language Acquisition 52

Chapter Six: Code Switching and Language Loss 57
Code Switching 58
Language Loss 60

Chapter Seven: English Learners with Disabilities or Other Special Needs 63
A Language Disorder Versus a Language Difference 64
Special Education Programs and English Learners 65
Coordinating Language and Communication Goals 68

Chapter Eight: Recommended Early Literacy Practices 71
Defining Early Literacy 72
Connecting Home and School Literacy Practices 73
Teaching Through Language 76
Reading Books Aloud to English Learners 77
Writing as a Part of Early Literacy 80
Making Stories Come Alive 81
Literacy Strategies for English Learners
    with Special Needs 83

Appendixes
A. Principles for Promoting Language, Literacy,
    and Learning for Preschool English Learners 91
B. Prekindergarten Learning and Development
    Guidelines 92
C. Desired Results for Children and Families 97
D. Transition to Kindergarten or Elementary School 100

Glossary 110

Works Cited 115

A Message from the State Superintendent of Public Instruction

Families, teachers, and policymakers have become increasingly aware of the need to address the linguistic diversity of California's preschool students, many of whom are experiencing formal schooling for the first time.

The teachers of preschool children have long been sensitive to the cultural backgrounds of the students and their families. Now they seek guidance as to how best to educate children from homes in which a language other than English is spoken and to prepare these English learners for their transition into kindergarten or elementary school.

This resource guide, *Preschool English Learners: Principles and Practices to Promote Language, Literacy, and Learning*, provides teachers with the knowledge and tools they seek to educate preschool English learners most effectively. It was developed by a group of experts who collectively brought strong practical, academic, and research backgrounds to the topic of educating young English learners. In their work the group demonstrated its steadfast commitment to assisting such children enrolled in California's schools and their families.

This document builds on the foundation laid by an earlier version titled *Fostering the Development of a First and a Second Language in Early Childhood*, published in 1998. In addition, companion materials, including a video, a Web site, and materials for statewide training, will be developed to supplement the information contained in the guide. This guide is meant to be used in conjunction with Appendix B, "Prekindergarten Learning and Development Guidelines," and Appendix C, "Desired Results for Children and Families," which can be found at the back of this publication.

I hope that teachers will find this resource guide useful as they work to provide high-quality preschool programs for all children. Thank you for your efforts on behalf of our children.

Jack O'Connell

Jack O'Connell
State Superintendent of Public Instruction

Acknowledgments

This publication was developed for the California Department of Education, Child Development Division, under the direction of **Rebeca Valdivia,** Director of the English Language Learning for Preschoolers Project, WestEd's Center for Child and Family Studies. This undertaking would not have been possible without the expertise and contributions of the many talented people who deserve our sincerest gratitude for their time, energy, and dedication. They include a panel of experts, staff from the California Department of Education's Child Development Division, staff from WestEd's Center for Child and Family Studies, and 50 focus-group participants from around the state representing the various audiences that the guide is designed to reach.

Panel of Experts

The panel of experts provided academic and practical perspectives affecting all aspects of the guide. Contributions to the contents, principles and practices, and updated research were generated by the panel during the 2003-04 contract year. Panel members and their job titles and locations are listed as follows:

Patricia Baquedano-Lopez, Associate Professor, Graduate School of Education, Language and Literacy, Society and Culture, University of California, Berkeley

Maria Fátima Castro, Coordinator, Central California Migrant Head Start, Santa Cruz County Office of Education, Capitola

Ruth Chao, Associate Professor, Department of Psychology, University of California, Riverside

Anna Eunhee Chee, Associate Professor, Charter College of Education, California State University, Los Angeles

Kris Gutierrez, Professor, Graduate School of Education, University of California, Los Angeles

J. Ronald Lally, Co-Director, Center for Child and Family Studies, WestEd, Sausalito

Peter Mangione, Co-Director, Center for Child and Family Studies, WestEd, Sausalito

Sy Dang Nguyen, Consultant, Child Development Division, California Department of Education, Sacramento

Joyce Palacio, Principal, El Sereno Early Education Center, Los Angeles Unified School District

James L. Rodriguez, Associate Professor, College of Education, San Diego State University

California Department of Education

Thanks are also extended to the following members of the Department's Child Development Division: **Michael Jett**, Director, whose vision and leadership inspired the development of the project; **Gwen Stephens**, Assistant Director, Quality Improvement and Capacity Building; and **Sy Dang Nguyen**, Consultant, for ongoing revisions and recommendations.

Project Staff

The writing, editing, and reviewing involved in any project cannot be completed without the tireless work of dedicated staff. The contributions of the following staff members from WestEd's Center for Child and Family Studies are gratefully acknowledged: **Peter Mangione**, for writing a considerable amount of the contents throughout the guide, editing multiple drafts, and providing administrative support, guidance, and oversight; **Carrie Parente**, for design, editorial, formatting, and administrative assistance; **Sara Webb**, for helping with the design and layout; and **J. Ronald Lally** and **Catherine Tsao**, Director, National and International Training, for proofreading.

Special Contributions

Special thanks go to **Marilyn Astore**, member of the Executive Committee, California Preschool Instructional Network. She reviewed several drafts of the guide, provided important recommendations concerning the presentation of content, especially in the chapter on early literacy, and contributed suggestions for resources and references.

Special thanks also go to **Joyce Palacio**, a member of the panel of experts, and **Norma Quan Ong**, an independent early childhood consultant in San Francisco. They contributed vignettes taken directly from children, families, and staff in early childhood settings.

Focus Groups

Four focus groups were assembled by WestEd in San Diego, San Francisco, El Centro, and Los Angeles. The 50 participants were preschool teachers, program directors from early childhood education programs, trainers, consultants, and parents. They examined an earlier draft of the guide and provided crucial feedback for improving its readability and accessibility for the target audience.

Editors

Rosario Diaz Greenberg, Associate Professor, California State University, San Marcos, and **James Rodriguez**, a member of the panel of experts, provided invaluable expertise during the extensive revision and editing process.

Photographs

The photographs in this guide came from two sources. **Julie Espinosa** and families in Pasadena, California, graciously contributed photographs. About half of the photographs were taken by Lang and Associates at the Educational Enrichment Systems, Inc./Linda Vista Child Development Center in San Diego. Many thanks are extended to **Mark Lang**, photographer, Director **Jennifer Anthony**, and the children, staff, and families at the center.

Introduction to the Resource Guide

Tucked away in one of the many multicultural communities in California is a state-funded child development program. There are 15 children in the class from Spanish-speaking, English-speaking, Vietnamese-speaking, Chinese-speaking, Farsi-speaking, and Russian-speaking homes. Many of the children have grown up together in this early care and education setting from the time they were infants. The lead teacher is bilingual in English and Farsi. Two assistants are bilingual in English and Spanish. There are also some roving staff members who are bilingual in Vietnamese and English and some who are bilingual in Chinese and English.

Engaged in a variety of activities, the children participate in small-group and whole-class instruction, individual projects, and adult-child interactions. Student needs, learning goals, and forms of assistance for each child are some of the factors the teacher has considered in planning the day's activities. The children use their home language and English to learn and to communicate in social interactions. The director and teacher explain that program planning has not been easy but that the ongoing attention to the children's language and literacy development in both their home language and English has been a key factor in the children's progressing in all areas of development as they move on to the class for four-year-olds in the following year.

What You Will Find in This Guide

This guide is designed to help the reader understand the preschool English learner more fully. Each chapter provides important information about the development, abilities, and everyday experiences of the preschool English learner that is based on current and rigorously conducted research. The preschool English learner is (1) a child whose first language is other than English and as a result is learning English as a second language; or (2) a child who is developing two or more languages, one of which may be English. During the preschool years from birth through five years of age, most children are still acquiring the basic knowledge of their home language, even when that language is English. The purpose of this guide is to enrich the reader's understanding of the language and literacy development of young English learners.

The primary audience for this guide is preschool teachers. The term *teacher* includes preschool classroom teachers, child development center teachers, and child care providers. Most of the information applies to family child care providers working with preschool English learners. This guide should be a starting point for you, the reader, to expand on what you already know about preschool children and gain insights into the unique strengths and needs of preschool English learners.

Core Beliefs

The following list of core beliefs should be considered as information is being presented in this guide. These beliefs stem from research and reflect an understanding of the challenges of educating preschool-age children, particularly English learners. Careful consideration of the beliefs will help preschool teachers focus on each child's experiences and circumstances as that child begins the journey toward the acquisition of academic English. Familiarity with these beliefs will also help teachers implement the information, principles, and practices presented in this guide. It is important to recognize that these beliefs are not mutually exclusive and that, in most instances, they overlap.

- *Understanding the English learner requires gathering as much information as possible about the child and his or her family and community.* Children grow and learn in the contexts of family, school, and community that often influence one another dynamically and interactively. Preschool educators can learn much from their observations of children's experiences in the multiple contexts of childhood (Bronfenbrenner 1979; Harrison and others 1990).

- *There is an important relationship between language, culture, and learning.* As children grow older, they become more proficient in the use of language, more culturally knowledgeable, and more competent in learning. Language allows children to learn more about their family's culture and the world. At the same time culture provides children with a lens that influences how they experience the world and how they learn (Gutierrez and Rogoff 2003; Vasquez, Pease-Alvarez, and Shannon 1994).

- *Language is a tool for learning.* Children's language is an essential tool enabling them to learn about the world around them. Home language and English are tools children use to learn everything from the cultural practices within the home to the academic content of the classroom (Gutierrez and Rogoff 2003).

- *There are multiple paths to childhood bilingualism.* Just as children's everyday experiences may differ from one another, children may follow different paths to developing more than one language. There is not a single best path to bilingualism. This diversity in achieving bilingualism reflects overall development whereby children may develop specific abilities at different times and at different rates (Hakuta 1986).

- *Language development and learning are shaped by children's experiences.* Children acquire skills and strategies and ways of doing things from the people around them as the children carry out everyday tasks and activities. They learn the appropriate use of language and literacy from experts (adults and other competent children) in their communities.

- *Second-language acquisition is a complex process.* Children take different paths, go through certain stages at different rates, and use various strategies in acquiring more than one language.

- *Acquiring oral language fluency in English differs from acquiring academic English, the formal language of the school.* Children use English within different contexts for different purposes. As a result children may use different varieties of English in the home, in the classroom, and on the playground. Academic English used in formal schooling may take longer to acquire than English used with other children in social circumstances, such as on the playground.

- *Being able to communicate in more than one language empowers children in a multicultural society.* Bilingualism is a valuable skill that allows children to use more than one language to experience the world and learn about it (Valdés 2003).

Principles and Practices: Children as Active Learners

In addition to the core beliefs that provide a foundation for this guide, a series of principles and practices is introduced throughout to promote language development, literacy, and learning among preschool English learners, including English learners with disabilities or other special needs. The use of the information, principles, and practices described will increase opportunities for growth and learning among English learners. These opportunities are vital to promoting the children's success in school and in life.

Throughout the guide the expansion of the English learner's acquisition of learning practices and abilities is emphasized. Achieving academic success in school includes developing a knowledge and mastery of formal schooling practices in addition to building on one's home or community language practices. All children can have high levels of achievement if provided with a rich, challenging curriculum and appropriate forms of assistance. When implemented, the information contained in this resource guide will help preschool English learners reach their fullest potential.

The core beliefs introduced earlier in this chapter are extended to principles and practices that incorporate the wide range of ways in which children can participate in numerous activities in their homes, schools, and communities. As with all other children, the development of English learners depends on a number of factors and influences that exist within those settings. For English learners in particular, such factors and influences would include the status given to their home language, the extent to which their communities and school programs embrace bilingualism, and the supports available to continue developing their first language as they develop fluency in English.

Children use a wide range of skills, strategies, and behaviors daily to develop linguistic, academic, and social competencies that facilitate the children's emerging ability to participate in the activities of their families, schools, neighborhoods, and communities. Variation among these contexts leads to variation in the language, literacy, and learning tools that children acquire and bring to the preschool context. The more preschool teachers know about how children learn, the better prepared the teachers will be to develop rich learning contexts. As preschool educators continue through this guide, they should think of children as active learners who draw on their previous knowledge and experiences to make sense of their world.

Summary of the Guide by Chapter

A central goal of this resource guide is to emphasize the importance of understanding the dynamic forces that shape development and learning among preschool English learners. In this chapter a set of core beliefs has been presented for consideration in implementing the principles and practices introduced throughout the guide. An overall theme that runs through these core beliefs is that developing a fuller understanding of the English learner is an important first step in thinking about and creating effective learning contexts that maximize children's language and literacy learning. A summary of the central points of each of the remaining chapters in the guide is presented as follows:

- *Chapter Two* describes English learners in California and discusses the crucial role that family members play in the language and literacy development of English learners. The ways in which home, school, and community contexts influence language development and literacy practices are also explained.

- *Chapter Three* continues to explore the various factors that often affect language development and literacy among English learners. Among those factors are the literacy skills children bring from their home language and the kinds of literacy practices in which they participate.

- *Chapter Four* describes the various paths to bilingualism, and *Chapter Five* provides an overview of how second-language acquisition occurs. The role that language plays in the process of learning is emphasized. Children acquire and use language as a tool to participate with others in their everyday activities across many contexts.

- *Chapter Six* presents the concept of code switching, by which a child can move back and forth between two or more languages. The chapter once again highlights the finding that children's language and literacy development is influenced by factors within the child's family, school, and community.

- *Chapter Seven* discusses working with English learners who have disabilities or other special needs, although most of the strategies suggested in other chapters can also be effective with this population. The reverse is also true; that is, many of the strategies for children with disabilities or other special needs are effective with English learners and preschoolers in general.

- *Chapter Eight* presents a set of recommended literacy practices for English learners. Because, like all other children, English learners have a range of interests and are motivated to participate in many different kinds of learning activities, they should be assigned literacy activities that allow them to learn about many different topics across a number of contexts. Being able to read influences a child's ability to write and vice versa, and literacy activities that allow young children to take on roles as both emergent readers and writers increase literacy development significantly.

Continued Professional Development

Although this guide provides an up-to-date, comprehensive discussion of preschool English learners, information on this topic is continually expanding and changing. Books have been written on the topics covered in each of the chapters. The guide provides references, resources, and thought-provoking questions to support continued professional development and a foundation for building on current

knowledge. To understand and serve the preschool English learner more fully, teachers should engage in intensive professional development, including coaching and mentoring.

Key to the Resource Guide

Throughout this guide various categories are used to present information in a different yet accessible manner. Each category has a different purpose and is represented by the following icons:

Research Highlights. Current research related to key topics being presented and discussed. One or more references for additional information are provided.

Principles and Practices. Instructional strategies teachers can implement in their classrooms and with families to educate the preschool English learner more effectively. Each principle provides the rationale for the practices that follow.

 Voices from the Preschool Classroom. Voices of teachers, children, and families that exemplify the concept or idea being discussed.

Research to Practice. Examples of curriculum and instructional practices derived directly from research.

Ask Yourself

1. Do I look at each of my students as an individual who brings competencies to the learning situation or as a member of a group or category, such as English learners?

2. Am I familiar with how our program applies proven approaches on first- and second-language development and learning?

Additional References

Early Childhood Head Start Task Force, U.S. Department of Education and U.S. Department of Health and Human Services. 2002. *Teaching Our Youngest: A Guide for Preschool Teachers and Child Care and Family Providers.* http://www.ed.gov/pubs/edpubs.html

Eastern Stream Center on Resources and Training. 2003. *Help! They Don't Speak English Starter Kit: A Resource Guide for Educators of Limited English Proficient Migrant Students, Grades Pre-K–6.* Oneonta, N.Y. Available at 1-800-451-8058. http://www.escort.org

Starting Points for Educators of Culturally and Linguistically Diverse Children 3 to 8 (video training series). Program 1: "I Don't Know Where to Start" (2002), Program 2: "Getting Your Message Across" (2002), and Program 3: "Bringing Language Alive!" (2003). Beaverton, Ore.: Educational Productions. http://www.edpro.com

Note: See pages 115–28 for a list of works cited in this publication.

Preschool English Learners, Their Families, and Their Communities

When asked how he successfully communicates with two- and three-year-old children who have had limited exposure to English, a monolingual English-speaking teacher replied: "It's all about relationships. Children respond to a calm voice and a comforting hug. I've learned a few simple phrases in Spanish to reassure children that they are safe while at our center. I also ask for help from the children who are learning English. In no time at all, I don't have to ask, for they automatically translate for the younger children. Translating for the teacher makes them feel special and makes learning two languages take on greater significance."

Chapter 2

Preschool
English Learners,
Their Families,
and Their
Communities

The Children

Recent demographic trends have far-reaching implications for early childhood educators. By the year 2030 children of European American families will make up less than 50 percent of the population under age five (Shonkoff and Phillips 2000).[1] Like many of the other states, California is becoming increasingly culturally, ethnically, and linguistically diverse. Latinos make up nearly 30 percent of the state's population; Asians, 9.1 percent; and African Americans, 7 percent (U.S. Bureau of the Census 2004).

For the 2005-06 school year, California school districts reported a total of more than 1.5 million English learners enrolled in kindergarten through grade twelve. That figure represents about 25 percent of California's 6.3 million students (California Department of Education 2006). However, the representation of English learners is even greater in the lower grades, including preschool, where more than one-third of all children attending public school speak a language other than English at home. As general public school enrollment has risen by at least 50 percent in the last two decades in California, the number of English learners has increased six times as much, as illustrated in Figure 1. As stated in Shonkoff and Phillips (2000, 65), "The changing

---

[1] The term *European American* is used in this publication to designate families of European origin living in the United States. Other designations found in the literature that are sometimes used interchangeably are *Caucasian, white,* and, occasionally, *mainstream.*

FIGURE 1. K–12 Enrollment and Percentage of English Learners in California, 1981–2006

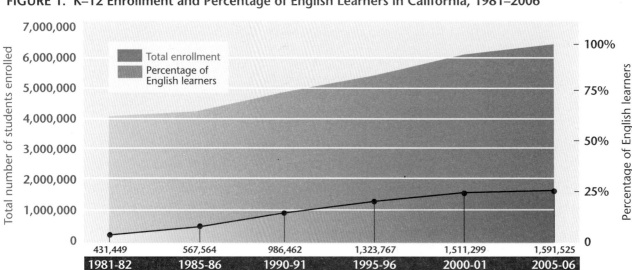

	1981-82	1985-86	1990-91	1995-96	2000-01	2005-06
	431,449	567,564	986,462	1,323,767	1,511,299	1,591,525

Source: California Department of Education.

demographics of the early childhood population in the United States present both the opportunity and the challenge of a great social experiment."

Because 40 percent of the nation's immigrant children (i.e., those under eighteen years of age) reside in California (U.S. Bureau of the Census 2003), a dramatic increase in culturally and linguistically diverse children attending California preschool programs has occurred. Figure 2 shows the number of preschool children ages three to five in California who were not enrolled in kindergarten, and Figure 3 shows the number of preschool children enrolled in public preschool and nursery programs.

Chapter 2
Preschool
English Learners,
Their Families,
and Their
Communities

FIGURE 2. Number of California Children Ages Three to Five Not Enrolled in Kindergarten, 2000

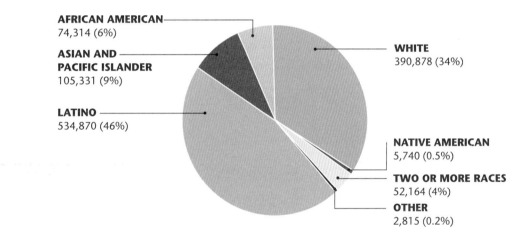

AFRICAN AMERICAN
74,314 (6%)

ASIAN AND
PACIFIC ISLANDER
105,331 (9%)

LATINO
534,870 (46%)

WHITE
390,878 (34%)

NATIVE AMERICAN
5,740 (0.5%)

TWO OR MORE RACES
52,164 (4%)

OTHER
2,815 (0.2%)

Source: California Research Bureau, California State Library, using the IPUMS 2000 (5% sample).

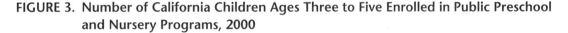

FIGURE 3. Number of California Children Ages Three to Five Enrolled in Public Preschool and Nursery Programs, 2000

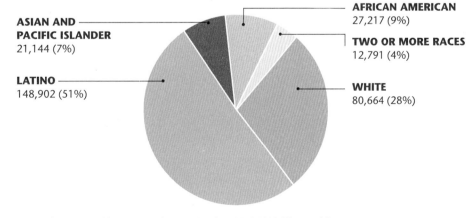

ASIAN AND
PACIFIC ISLANDER
21,144 (7%)

LATINO
148,902 (51%)

AFRICAN AMERICAN
27,217 (9%)

TWO OR MORE RACES
12,791 (4%)

WHITE
80,664 (28%)

Source: California Research Bureau, California State Library, using the IPUMS 2000 (5% sample).

Chapter 2

Preschool
English Learners,
Their Families,
and Their
Communities

The California Department of Education collects data on 56 languages spoken by children and their families in the state (California Department of Education 2006). The most prevalent languages besides English are Spanish, Vietnamese, Cantonese, Hmong, Pilipino (Tagalog), and Korean, as shown in Table 1.

TABLE 1. Most Prevalent Non-English Languages and Number of K–12 Students Speaking Those Languages in California, 1980–2006

Rank	1980-81	1990-91	2000-01	2005-06
1	SPANISH 285,567	SPANISH 755,359	SPANISH 1,259,954	SPANISH 1,341,369
2	VIETNAMESE 22,826	VIETNAMESE 40,477	VIETNAMESE 37,978	VIETNAMESE 34,263
3	CANTONESE 14,196	CANTONESE 21,498	HMONG 27,124	CANTONESE 22,756
4	KOREAN 7,508	HMONG 21,060	CANTONESE 25,089	HMONG 21,907
5	PILIPINO (TAGALOG) 6,752	KHMER (CAMBODIAN) 20,055	PILIPINO (TAGALOG) 18,157	PILIPINO (TAGALOG) 20,556
6	LAO 5,586	PILIPINO (TAGALOG) 18,146	KOREAN 16,874	KOREAN 16,091

Source: California Department of Education.

To find out what language or languages a child is learning, the questioner must determine what language is spoken in the home and whether more than one language is spoken. Making assumptions based on the child's last name does not always determine accurately the child's home language. For example, a Spanish last name may not indicate that Spanish is the language spoken in the home. Some children and families that have Spanish last names may speak only English. On the other hand many immigrants come to the U.S. from indigenous populations in Latin America and have Spanish last names but may speak indigenous languages rather than Spanish. Among the most common languages spoken in California by children of these immigrants are Zapotec, Mixtec, Quechua, and a number of Mayan languages. Still other families come from different countries formerly under Spanish rule, such as the Philippines, and may have Spanish last names but speak other languages, such as Tagalog, French, or Creole.

The Role of Families in Language and Literacy Development

Just as there is widespread diversity in the children attending preschool programs, so is there diversity in their families. Families differ in the configuration of members, language dominance, values, goals, and childrearing practices as well as immigration, migration, and acculturation experiences.

Researchers have demonstrated the positive effects of parental involvement on children's achievement in school (Booth and Dunn 1996). Much of that research has been centered on European American families. Now there is a growing interest in examining which practices are best suited for culturally and linguistically diverse families, including those who have recently immigrated to this country (Buriel and De Ment 1997; Valdés 1996). Today, teachers, programs, and communities are continually exploring ways to partner with families because they recognize that families have a wealth of knowledge and experiences that can serve as valuable resources in their children's education.

Some families of preschool children have been in the United States for several generations, and other families may have older children who have been part of the school system for several years. Both may be quite familiar with their roles as partners in their children's education.

Teachers and family members may experience differences in language and culture that lead to challenges in forming effective partner-

ships. Different expectations regarding the role of parents and teachers in children's education, unfamiliarity with the school system, and prior experiences with school staff can lead to misunderstandings between teachers and families. For instance, parents are sometimes baffled when asked to give their opinion about what is happening in the classroom. They feel that such matters are the responsibility not of the parents but of the teachers. Some immigrant parents may also feel intimidated by their lack of knowledge of the school system. Addressing these potential differences carefully and respectfully can greatly improve home-school partnerships.

Chapter 2

Preschool
English Learners,
Their Families,
and Their
Communities

The Diversity of the Immigration Experience

The experience of leaving one's home country and moving to a new country is referred to as a family's *immigration experience*. This process can be exciting and positive for some families and a difficult and challenging one for others, with many families encountering both positive and negative experiences as part of their immigration to the United States. The preschool teacher can be more sensitive to a child's adjustment and performance in the classroom by learning about the family's journey (Igoa 1995).

Some families that come to the United States as immigrants have had time to plan for their move. For example, a child's parents may have arranged for a secure job on arrival. Or a family may have moved to a community with an established base of support for immigrants, possibly even relatives, from their country or region. Those families will likely adjust to their new surroundings more easily than will families that lack such support.

Families that have to leave their country of origin suddenly and involuntarily do not have the luxury of preparing for the move. They are missing the needed emotional preparation of imagining life in their new country (Suarez-Orozco and Suarez-Orozco 2001). Perhaps a family had to flee suddenly under traumatic circumstances or had to live in refugee camps or crowded, makeshift shelters. Or a family may have had to separate, with some members going to the child's current city of residence and others to a different location or country. Having arrived in the United States, they may face the anxiety of searching for employment and experiencing isolation.

In short, many factors play a role in a family's immigration to the United States, and those factors often affect the immigration experience and the transition to life in this country. A key part of the transition for many immigrant children and their families is the acquisition of a new language and adjustment to school.

Connecting School and the Home Language

Some families may be well informed about language development and bilingualism and have definite language goals for their children. Consequently, they enroll their children in preschool programs that reinforce the family's home language or are designed as bilingual preschool programs.

Chapter 2

Preschool
English Learners,
Their Families,
and Their
Communities

Other families may enroll their children in local language classes (e.g., in Saturday schools in many Asian communities) to develop or maintain their home language (Fishman 2001). Other settings that support the maintenance of the home language include participation in religious activities and services, community events and festivals, and other children's programs and activities.

Other families may not have given much thought to language acquisition before enrolling their children in preschool programs. For example, families with children who have identified disabilities may still be trying to understand their children's diagnoses, the workings of special education, and the different types of programs available. They may also be sorting out how the disabilities will affect the children's language development. In any case, conversations with each family regarding language learning, language goals, language resources, and a program's philosophy of language will be a valuable and necessary part of their children's success in school and at home.

Children's learning improves when they can communicate at home what they have learned at school. When children are given the tools to do so, teachers are fostering closer communication between home and school. Children need to master the words of both the school language and the home language to explain school activities. Because the amount of home language used at school may differ from program to program and from classroom to classroom, children should, whenever possible, be helped to develop a working vocabulary in the home language so that they can discuss school activities in which English has been spoken.

> **TEACHER**
>
> At conference time I like children to show their journals to their parents. It is a great way for young children to share their own work and progress, over time, with their families. It is rewarding, for both me and the parents, to see the dictation move from the child's home language to English. I hear children 'reading' the English dictation to their parent and then translating so their parent will understand. This is also the beginning of what we hope will be a lifelong dialogue between parent and child about school, homework, and learning.

Chapter 2

Preschool
English Learners,
Their Families,
and Their
Communities

PRINCIPLES AND PRACTICES

1

PRINCIPLE

The education of English learners is enhanced when preschool programs and families form meaningful partnerships.

Family (parent) involvement and participation are improved when families are valued contributors as planners, trainers, and evaluators of their children's educational programs. Teachers should recognize and respect families' language beliefs and practices to develop a more comprehensive understanding of the language development of English learners.

PRACTICES

- Determine how language learning, home language support, and communication goals will be addressed in your setting for all students, including students with disabilities.

- Acknowledge the many responsibilities that parents and families discharge daily.

- Highlight the many ways in which families are already involved in their children's education.

- Provide options for home-based activities that can support what children are learning at school.

- Share and model the belief that the involvement of parents in their children's education, accompanied by high educational expectations, results in better long-term academic and social-emotional development.

- Provide opportunities for parents and family members to share their skills with staff, the children in the program, and other families.

- Allow family members to determine how they would like to be supported and generate ideas for ways in which they can both lead and implement those supports.

- Provide specific information regarding program expectations, academic standards, and transition to kindergarten.

- Hold an open house or potluck dinner for families in the program.

Chapter 2

Preschool
English Learners,
Their Families,
and Their
Communities

Varieties of Language

Longitudinal studies of children growing up in bilingual communities support the notion that young children use language for different social and cognitive purposes and learn not just languages but different registers of those languages. Language *registers* are the different forms of the same language used with certain people or in certain situations. For example, children may use the formal register to speak to parents, elders, or teachers and child care providers and the informal register in other social settings, such as at the playground, with siblings, and with other children at a child care center. They may also address individuals entirely in one language or register but not in the other.

Children live in language-rich environments where they communicate with their parents, siblings, peers, and other caregivers. Those environments might include both the home language (formal and informal registers) and English. A variety of English, *academic English,* is the language of books used at school and that spoken by teachers, administrators, and many students.

Given the vast number of opportunities to come into contact with other varieties of English—at the playground or at stores, for example—children may have been exposed to those forms of English and may have already incorporated words or forms from these varieties into their language repertoires. Each variety of English or any other language has its purpose and is preferred in certain contexts. Therefore, it is important to communicate to children that their proficiency in English other than academic English is useful in many situations.

RESEARCH HIGHLIGHTS

Zentella's 1997 study of Puerto Rican children growing up in New York City provides an example of the varieties of registers that children can employ creatively in response to their communities' historical experiences of migration and language contact. In her analysis of children's speech, Zentella identifies a number of varieties of Spanish and English used by the children. Language development in this community reflected the social setting in which children lived. Contact with members from other cultural and linguistic groups (for example, African American English speakers) also influenced the language repertoires of these young bilingual children.

Chapter 2

Preschool
English Learners,
Their Families,
and Their
Communities

Explaining the value of knowing more than one register or language can be done in a developmentally appropriate manner, just as teachers explain equity, skin color, and disability to young children. Learning academic English will lead to improved success in school and other formal contexts.

Ask Yourself

1. What can I do to become more aware of a student's previous experiences?

2. For those students who are immigrants, how much awareness do I have of their immigrant experience?

3. How can I provide a nurturing environment where children from different cultural and linguistic backgrounds can feel safe to practice new words or use a new language?

4. How do I show the children and their families that I value their home language?

5. How familiar am I with the many language and literacy practices of my students and their families?

Additional References

Alma, A., and C. Baker. 2001. *Guía Para Padres y Maestros de Niños Bilingües*. Clevedon, England: Multilingual Matters.

Ballanger, C. 1999. *Teaching Other People's Children: Literacy and Learning in a Bilingual Classroom*. New York: Teachers College Press.

Lee, S. 2006. "Using Children's Texts to Communicate with Parents of English-Language Learners," *Young Children*, Vol. 61, No. 5, 18–25.

Note: See pages 115–28 for a list of works cited in this publication.

Connecting First
and Second Languages

Teacher: "Jorge, can you tell me your story in English or Spanish because you're bilingual?

Jorge: "What is bilingual?"

Teacher: "Bilingual is when you are able to speak in two languages."

Jorge: "I can speak two languages. I'm bilingual!"

Second child: "Teacher, teacher, I'm bilingual too! I speak English and Spanish!"

Jorge: "I want to speak three languages! I want to learn Chinese so I can talk to my friend next door to my house."

Teacher: "People who speak three languages are trilingual. Let's ask Mrs. Cheung if she'll teach us some words in Chinese."

Children and Their Language Development

The purpose of language is to communicate needs, thoughts, and feelings and to share meaning with others, as demonstrated in the teacher-student dialogue just quoted. Even before they can say their first words, infants are immersed in a world of language and communicate nonverbally through facial expressions, tone of voice, volume, and gestures. For instance, infants who hold up both arms may be communicating nonverbally that they want to be picked up.

Toward the end of the first year, infants start responding to spoken word cues and try to play "peek-a-boo" or "pat-a-cake" and may wave "bye-bye." They are taking in more and more language. As they begin to comprehend, they are preparing the way for speech. But before they can speak the names of things, they alter their gaze or hand things to others to show that they understand the names.

A child's first words help the child obtain things and cause adults to act in various ways. Naming things becomes a game, and the child echoes and repeats words. Sometimes it is difficult to understand just what the child is trying to say. Adults need to listen closely, watching for nonverbal signs and guessing to understand the child and to respond correctly.

Young children's early speech is *telegraphic,* meaning that, as with telegrams, which are abbreviated communications, children omit many words because of their limited ability to express and remember large pieces of information. Young children include the most important words in their telegraphic phrases, as in "Mommy shoe." However, it may be difficult to guess exactly what is missing. Is it "I want Mommy's shoe?" Or is it "Mommy's shoe is on the floor?" As their intellectual capacities increase, children eventually learn to add more words to clarify the meaning of their expressions.

As children grow older, their use of language becomes increasingly creative. The word "no," for example, occurs with persistent frequency. For some children "no" initially indicates that something or someone is not present or does not exist. "No dada" means that daddy is not home or not in the room where the child can see him. Soon, "no" may come to mean rejection or denial. A child using three or more words together may say, "No want eat peas." Eventually, "no" is inserted in the sentence but perhaps not where it belongs, as in "Johnny want no go bath." The last stage is proper usage, as in "No, I do not want a book."

During the preschool years children are continually developing their language. A particularly interesting aspect of first-language acquisition is the similarity in that development from child to child. For example, as children learn to form noun and verb endings in English, most go through a stage in which they say "foots" instead of "feet," "goed" instead of "went," and "mines" instead of "mine." These creative uses of language are a part of normal language development and show that the children are trying to figure out the patterns or rules that govern language. The expressions are called *overgeneralizations;* that is, children are applying a rule or pattern too broadly, such as forming a plural by adding "s" so that "foot" becomes "foots."

Most three-year-old children throughout the world can:

- Communicate effectively their needs to others around them.
- Produce talk that follows the grammatical patterns of the languages spoken around them.
- Articulate most of the sounds of their language(s) and put those sounds together according to the rules of the language(s).
- Use a large vocabulary that may contain words from each of the languages they hear.
- Continue to learn new words at an amazing rate.
- Understand the purposes of language, make statements, ask questions, issue demands, and make requests.
- Use language in socially appropriate situations.
- Use language creatively and productively to convey original thoughts and ideas.
- Engage in language activities that are valued in their cultural groups (e.g., greeting, storytelling, teasing, singing, debating).
- Be exposed to and have a number of learning experiences in using their home language and quite possibly other language varieties spoken around them.

Although the process of learning a language is similar for most children, each child progresses at his or her own rate. Some children do not say their first words until they are two years old; others at the same age are putting together two, three, or more words. However, as discussed earlier, all children have many ways to communicate, such as babbling, gesturing, changing facial expressions, offering toys and objects, and changing their tone of voice or pitch of their cry, even when they may not yet be able to express themselves in words.

The Components of Language

Babies are born with a capacity to learn any language. That capacity does not decrease as they fine-tune their home language on the way to mastering it. Young children experiment with language much as scientists do. They hypothesize and make predictions, draw conclusions based on patterns or rules of language from their understanding, and try out their findings. In learning to talk, children accomplish a great many things. Principally, they learn the following:

- *The Sound System (Phonology).* The rule system within a language by which phonemes or units of sound are connected to make words is known as *phonology.* Babies are born with the capacity to make the sounds in any of the world's languages. It takes time for children to learn how to make the sounds of their language correctly and for the muscles used in speech to mature. For that reason a young child whose home language is English may say "pway" instead of "play." Gradually, the child's speech becomes increasingly adult-like.

- *The Structure of Words (Morphology). Morphology* refers to the rules for how meaningful units of language are put together to form syllables and words. Young children learning English as their first language start out with simple morpheme or syllable combinations, such as "da-da," "ma-ma," or "ne-ne." Later, they use more adult-like pronunciations, such as "daddy," "mommy," and "Nelly."

Parts of Oral and Sign Language System

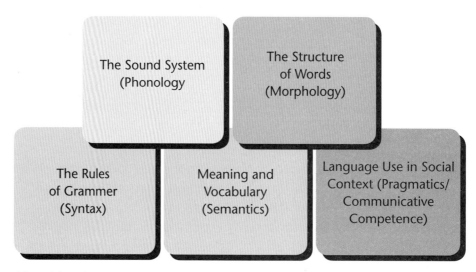

Adapted from "Even Start Research-based Early Childhood and Parenting Education Professional Development, 2003," California Department of Education, Sacramento.

- *The Rules of Grammar (Syntax).* All languages have rules for how words are put together to form sentences, otherwise known as *syntax*. Children learn to follow the rules of their home language gradually and at times may apply them incorrectly. A two-year-old English speaker might say, "I no want candy." But in time such language usage no longer occurs.

- *Meaning and Vocabulary (Semantics).* The study of the meanings of words and phrases is known as *semantics*. Learning the various meanings that can be expressed in a language is a lifetime task. Children learn to label objects and to develop concepts through verbal and nonverbal interactions with persons around them. As they mature, their understanding of concepts becomes more refined. For example, at one point "doggie" might refer to a horse, a cow, or a dog because all are four-footed. Eventually, "doggie" takes on the meaning understood by older persons.

- *Language Use in Social Context (Pragmatics/ Communicative Competence).* The system of rules and conventions, both unstated and stated, for using spoken language, along with forms of nonverbal communication appropriate within different social contexts, has been referred to as *pragmatics* and more recently as *communicative competence*. Children have to learn the ways in which language is used in many different situations. In developing their communicative competence, children realize that language can have many functions. Some of the major functions of language by which children demonstrate communicative competence are the following (Hamayan and Perlman 1990; Kasper and Rose 2003; LoCastro 2003):

1. *Imparting and seeking factual information*
    a. Identifying things
    b. Reporting about things, using description or narrative
    c. Asking for or correcting factual information

RESEARCH HIGHLIGHTS

Learning the meanings of concepts and objects takes longer than learning labels for them. For example, learning that a cute furry animal is called a "cat" takes longer and is more difficult than recognizing that the word "cat" and "*gato*" (Spanish for cat) refer to the same thing (Peynircioglu and Durgunoglu 1993; Peynircioglu and Tekcan 1993).

2. *Expressing and finding out intellectual attitudes*
   a. Expressing agreement and disagreement
   b. Accepting or declining an offer or invitation
   c. Stating whether one knows or does not know something or someone
   d. Giving and seeking permission to do something

3. *Expressing and finding out emotional attitudes*
   a. Expressing wants, desires, likes, interests, preferences, intentions (and their opposites, such as dislikes)
   b. Expressing surprise, hope, satisfaction, fear, worry, sympathy, and disappointment

4. *Expressing and finding out moral attitudes*
   a. Forgiving and apologizing
   b. Expressing approval or disapproval
   c. Expressing appreciation, regret, or indifference

5. *Getting things done*
   a. Suggesting a course of action
   b. Asking, inviting, advising, instructing, or directing others to do or not to do something
   c. Offering or requesting help

6. *Socializing*
   a. Meeting, greeting, and saying goodbye to people
   b. Attracting attention
   c. Congratulating
   d. Beginning a meal

As children mature, they learn how to use language differently with different people in school and in their home environments. They learn how commands, requests, and statements with subtle differences in structure, such as "We haven't been to the park for a long time now," can be more effective in certain situations than "I want to go to the park," according to content and intention. When children employ a different phrase to achieve a particular goal with a certain person at a specific point in time, they are showing fairly advanced knowledge of social interaction and communication.

In schools, however, the focus of the curriculum tends to be primarily on imparting and seeking factual information. As a result, teachers may unintentionally be overlooking children's many other language and communication skills.

A Wide Range of Language Practices

In addition to finding individual differences in the rate of learning language, researchers have identified cultural differences in the way in which language is acquired and used. For some children language development is assisted through interactions with props, such as books, toys, and stuffed animals. Even before children can talk, adults in some families often question the children and interact with them orally, labeling and describing what is happening:

"But this baby wants to go to sleep, doesn't he?"

"Yes. See those little eyes are getting heavy."

This interaction does not happen in all cultures or even in all segments of our society. A poor community in South Carolina studied by Heath (1983) provides an example of an American community in which children live in an environment without language-teaching props. Although these children were surrounded by a rich, constant stream of speech, Heath found that little attention was given to their attempts to verbalize. Cooing and babbling noises were ignored, and no attempt was made to interpret the children's early sounds. Yet the development of speech in these children occurred at the same rate as that of middle-class children. The children in the study simply followed a different route. They learned to speak by imitating the ends of overheard phrases or sentences, gradually building up longer speech patterns until they could get attention and enter into conversation.

Mother (talking to neighbor with child nearby): "But they won't call back. Won't happen."

Child: "Call back."

Neighbor: "Sam's going over there Saturday; he'll pick up a form."

Child: "Pick up 'on, pick up 'on."

RESEARCH HIGHLIGHTS

Research across language and cultural groups indicates that throughout the world family and community members interact with babies and young children in many different ways:

- Among European-American families "motherese" or "parentese" is commonly heard among adults interacting with very young children.

- In other communities children are sometimes not seen as full-fledged conversational partners and may not often be spoken to directly (Ochs and Schieffelin 1984).

- Among the Kaluli of New Guinea, parents are very conscious of language development and deliberately try to teach young children to speak. They use direct instruction, telling children appropriate things to say in specific circumstances. The speech they use—and expect children to use—is normal adult speech (Schieffelin 1979).

Because not all children have had the same experiences in learning how to talk, they may have different expectations about how they should interact with adults or other children. The "Research to Practice: The Use of Questions" that follows demonstrates why it is important for teachers to become familiar with the different experiences and practices of their students.

Although some similarities within a cultural or language group may occur in childrearing and communication practices, the manner in which those practices occur may vary significantly among individuals and families.

Preschool programs in the United States are typically structured to operate according to a well-established school culture. In their classrooms children from different cultural and linguistic backgrounds may experience cultural conflicts because the children are accustomed to different ways of learning and communicating.

RESEARCH TO PRACTICE

The Use of Questions

In schools across America teachers may ask known-answer questions. For example, a teacher may ask a student what color the student's blouse is. The answer is already known. The student knows that her blouse is red in color. An example of an unknown-answer question would be for the teacher to ask what the student had for dinner the previous night because the teacher had not dined with the student.

Heath (1983) found that children used to being asked unknown-answer questions at home were baffled as to why teachers would ask known-answer questions when the response was usually so obvious and as result participated less in class.

Cazden (1988) suggests a way to apply this knowledge to a social studies lesson titled "Our Community":

- Use photographs of different sections of the local community; public buildings of the town and surrounding areas, such as the countryside; beaches; and so forth.

- Ask the children such questions as the following:

"What's happening here?"

"Have you ever been here?"

"Tell me what you did when you were there."

"What's this like (pointing to a scene or item in a scene)?"

As a result of using these types of questions, teachers may get more active and assertive and complete responses than if they had asked the students only the following:

"What kind of building is this?"

"Where is this located?"

PRINCIPLES AND PRACTICES

2

PRINCIPLE

Children benefit when their teachers understand cultural differences in language use and incorporate them into the daily routine.

Culturally responsive teaching practices in the preschool classroom create a positive learning environment. They incorporate the linguistic and cultural resources that children bring with them and thereby promote their learning and overall growth.

PRACTICES

- Structure activities so that children can engage in telling stories or recounting events by expressing themselves through various means, such as speech, pantomime, pointing, and role-playing.

- Remember that children benefit from experiencing different types of interactions with adults and with peers, including cooperative and peer-oriented activities as well as more independent activities.

- Inform family members, providers, teachers, and specialists about different types of language interaction practices used at school and by the families of the children in your class.

- Accept silence or quiet observation as a proper way for some children to participate, especially when they first join your class.

- Be aware that ways of expressing feelings, such as excitement, anger, happiness, frustration, and sadness, differ in various cultures. For example, children may show excitement by shouting and jumping for joy, by smiling and offering a coy look, by showing no outward signs while inwardly experiencing anticipation, or by sharing with a friend or a trusted adult the fact that they are excited.

- Note that children from different cultural backgrounds may interpret a single action by the teacher to have contrasting meanings. For example, a teacher may point to signal where she wants the children to go. But some children may think she is reprimanding them, singling them out for some reason, or saying she wants "one" of something (since she has one finger out).

- Vary wait time, the amount of time you allow children to respond. Children from certain cultural backgrounds find the pace of verbal interactions in U.S. schools very different from what they are accustomed to.

- Make sure that your classroom environment reflects the children's cultures and languages in each learning center; on walls, windows, and bulletin boards; and in educational and play materials.

- Visit the children's homes and observe not only how parents interact with the child but also how other relatives and siblings talk to the child and how the child talks to or interacts with them.

- Go to community functions attended by parents and children and other community members and observe the communication styles of the people attending those functions.

Awareness of How Language Works

Teachers can call attention to the task of learning a language by sharing with the children their own experiences in trying to learn another language. The children should know that learning a second language can be difficult and that people progress at different rates in learning both first and second languages. They need opportunities to verbalize their awareness of language differences and, most important, to learn that all languages are valuable. By making explicit this awareness of differences in language through conversations, such as the one found at the beginning of this chapter, teachers will provide children with concrete examples of the many uses of their language abilities and the benefits to be gained.

Another reason for children to have an early awareness of language and language differences is that many young children will become language brokers for family members and friends (if they have not already become brokers). As language brokers children can use their developing bilingual language skills to act as interpreters between institutions and family members and to assist peers or siblings who may not know as much English as they do.

CANTONESE-SPEAKING GRANDMOTHER

I take Karen (four and one-half years old) with me when I go shopping. She helps me because I don't speak any English. She translates for me on the bus and in the market and sometimes when I pay a bill. Sometimes I'm nervous when she's not with me. She is very confident.

RESEARCH HIGHLIGHTS

A study of students in grades five and six who translated for others illustrated the many ways in which bilingual children translated or interpreted and even paraphrased for others throughout their childhood years. These students used their remarkable everyday interpreting skills in schools, government offices, and hospitals, to name a few places (Faulstich Orellana 2003).

Children learning English as a second language often have more opportunities to be exposed to English-dominant environments than do their parents and older family members. However, in communicating to families what may be sensitive or personal information, preschool program staff should avoid using young children and rely instead on bilingual staff members, including trained interpreters. Further, teachers can avoid pressuring young children inadvertently to act as language brokers in inappropriate situations by adhering to the strategies described throughout this guide.

The Influence of Peers on Language Development

Interacting with peers in a preschool setting is advantageous for many developmental reasons, including opportunities to develop social skills and form identities. In collaborative peer activities children learn to negotiate goals and the meaning of the activities at hand. More experienced peers, those with more advanced mastery of the language, can also be effective language models for children who are newcomers to the community. In small-group and large-group activities with

(Continued on page 32)

3

PRINCIPLES AND PRACTICES

PRINCIPLE

Successful practices promote shared experiences in which language is used as a meaningful tool to communicate interests, ideas, and emotions.

A positive consequence of culturally responsive teaching practices is that the teacher's communication in the classroom is better received when children can relate to the language and content being presented. The children's ability to relate to classroom learning is further strengthened when the teacher supports the children's use of the home language while the children acquire English. By engaging in practices that promote learning through shared experiences, children become more competent bilingual-bicultural learners.

PRACTICES

- Introduce a vocabulary word by connecting it with related words in one or more of the children's languages. If you are not bilingual, access the bilingual abilities of other colleagues or family members. For example, after reading a story about the circus, connect the word *circus* with *el circo* (in Spanish) or *le cirque* (in French) and also connect *circus* with the word *circle* in English.

- Use the sign or picture symbol of a word for children with disabilities. Also use a voice-output device with a prerecorded label in the child's home language and in English.

- Maintain a consistent routine, along with a picture or photo schedule, so that, with a little observation, English learners (with and without disabilities) can pick up clues about what to do next.

- Demonstrate how to make requests, how to initiate conversations, and how to "take the floor."

- Present new vocabulary in a context that allows the children to determine the meaning rather than in isolation, as in lists of words. *Note:* Language should be learned in the context of the here and now. Whenever possible, use real items or toy versions, photographs, or drawings of the items.

- Promote and assist peer interactions to provide opportunities for English learners, including those with disabilities, to communicate with peers who are more fluent English speakers and can serve as language models.

- Keep language a step beyond the child's current development, but not too far. As the child's language develops, adults should gradually increase the complexity of their language.

their peers, children will benefit from the support in learning offered by their teachers. Group activities can be a key supplement to the social and cognitive development of children.

Ask Yourself

1. What can I do in my classroom to be more proactive about integrating culturally relevant practices in language use?

2. How can I adapt the curriculum to encourage multiple opportunities for peer interactions to support each child's language development?

3. How am I using the children's home languages so that the children can continue to learn concepts as they progress in learning English?

Additional References

Bowman, B. T.; M. S. Donovan; and M. S. Burns, editors. 2001. *Eager to Learn: Educating Our Preschoolers.* Washington, D.C.: National Academy Press.

Burns, M.S., and others. 1999. *Starting Out Right: A Guide to Promoting Children's Success.* Washington, D.C.: National Academy Press.

"The Child's Brain: Syllable from Sound." Program 2, The Secret Life of the Brain. PBS video series. http://www.pbs.org/wnet/brain/outreach/series_desc.html (accessed 12-29-05)

Gopnik, A.; A. Meltzoff; and P. Kuhl. 1999. *The Scientist in the Crib: Minds, Brains, and How Children Learn.* New York: William Morrow and Company.

Note: See pages 115–28 for a list of works cited in this publication.

Paths to Bilingualism

Kemin is four years old, and his sister Sofia is three years old. They were born in Southern California. Their mother, born in the United States, is of Mexican descent and is fluent in Spanish and English. Their father was born in China and came to the United States with his parents and two siblings when he was a teenager. He is fluent in Mandarin Chinese and in English. Kemin and Sofia have been learning Spanish from their mother, her extended family, and their babysitter and Chinese from their father and his extended family at a school offering instruction in Chinese on Saturdays. Now they are enrolled in preschool, where the teacher uses both English and Spanish as languages for instruction. Their teacher reports that the children's participation in her classroom is a reflection of each child's personality and temperament. Kemin is more reserved and prefers to stay close to the teacher or her assistant. Sofia is quite outgoing and assertive and is often leading activities or talking to friends. At preschool they are both making progress in their English and Spanish development as well as in all other areas of learning.

Most children throughout the world learn to speak two or more languages (Tucker 1999). Indeed, bilingualism is present in just about every country in the world, in all classes of society, and in all age groups (Grosjean 1982). This chapter is about children learning to speak more than one language.

Theoretical Basis for Supporting Bilingualism

Being exposed to more than one language during childhood can ease the transition from speaking and using the home language to acquiring a second language, usually English, for school. This transition is also known as *cross-language transfer* (August and Hakuta 1997; Ben-Zeev 1997; Bernhardt 1991; Durgunoglu and Verhoeven 1998). What research has shown to be successful in teaching older English learners can help in making decisions on curriculum and instruction for young English learners. Two major hypotheses that have been developed to explain the phenomenon of cross-language transfer, the interdependence hypothesis and the threshold hypothesis, are described as follows:

- The *interdependence hypothesis* (Cummins 1981, 1984) maintains that in developing proficiency in one language, children also develop underlying cognitive skills and metalinguistic awareness—awareness of the content and meaning of language rather than its external structure or sound. This universal understanding gained in acquiring one language facilitates learning and developing proficiency in a second language or in additional languages.

- A second hypothesis explaining cross-language transfer is the *threshold hypothesis* (Cummins and Swain 1986). This hypothesis

RESEARCH HIGHLIGHTS

There is general agreement that bilingualism leads to multiple advantages for children and adults. Some of the benefits of knowing more than one language are listed as follows (August and Hakuta 1997; Baker 2000a):

Communication advantages: wider communication networks; literacy in two languages; metalinguistic awareness

Cultural advantages: broader enculturation; deeper multiculturalism; two "language worlds" of experience; greater tolerance; less racism

Cognitive advantages: thinking; memory; brain plasticity

Character advantages: raised self-esteem; security in identity

Curriculum advantages: increased curriculum achievement and ease in learning a third language or additional languages

Cash and financial advantages: increased employment opportunities; resulting economic benefits

maintains that English learners must achieve minimum thresholds (levels) of proficiency in both their home language and English before they can achieve the benefits of bilingualism. Studies indicate that bilingual students who are proficient in their first language have higher academic achievement in English and other subjects than do those students who are not proficient (Thomas and Collier 2003a; Yeung, Marsh, and Suliman 2000). This finding, which supports the threshold hypothesis, has prompted researchers to state that a high level of proficiency in a first language is more likely than not to assist students in acquiring a second language.

Linguists and psychologists generally agree that children reach proficiency in their first language by the age of five, assuming no identified risk factors are involved. Children acquire the speech patterns of those around them, learning the rules of grammar, gaining a large vocabulary, and learning to use language appropriately in social contexts.

Most children without learning difficulties succeed in acquiring a first language, but not all children are successful in acquiring a second language. Mastering a second language depends in great part on the interaction of external and internal factors. External factors may include access to speakers of a second language, the frequency with which children come into contact with and interact with those speakers, the degree to which the second-language context is emotionally supportive, and the messages and pressures present in school and society regarding the mastery of the second language. Internal factors may include the children's cognitive abilities and limitations, perceived need to learn a second language, talent in learning language, and individual temperaments and social skills. If the children's home and school communities value bilingualism, then children will likely learn and maintain both of their languages at high levels (Winsler and others 1999).

By implementing the many practices included in this guide, preschool teachers will be able to honor and value a child's home language and culture while English is being introduced. Indeed, the questions of when and how much English is to be introduced in the preschool years require a great deal of thought and consultation with family members and educators knowledgeable about second-language acquisition.

A child becomes bilingual in different ways, primarily through the simultaneous acquisition of two languages or the successive acquisition of a second language. Both refer to the child's exposure to a second language. For some children exposure begins at a very early age; for others it occurs later. A rule of thumb is that exposure to two languages before the age of three may lead to *simultaneous bilingualism,* which means that the children are learning two languages at once. Because children acquire most aspects of oral or spoken language by the age of three, the introduction of a new language after that age leads to *successive bilingualism.* The quality and quantity of exposure to both languages and the opportunities or tendencies children have to use both languages, together or separately, lead to different paths for second-language acquisition.

Simultaneous Bilingualism

Simultaneous bilingualism (also known as simultaneous language acquisition, simultaneous second-language acquisition, or dual-language acquisition) applies to children who develop two languages equally or nearly equally through exposure to both and frequent opportunities to use both. Some children in preschool programs have already been exposed to two languages and use both at developmentally appropriate levels. For example, some children speak Tagalog with their parents and older relatives and English with their siblings and friends.

Bilingual children learning two languages at the same time may not have had the same amount of exposure or opportunities to use each of the languages. A bilingual person with a perfectly balanced knowledge of both languages is rare, for life experiences in each language are seldom duplicated.

Children acquiring two languages simultaneously follow developmental phases similar to those for children acquiring the languages separately. (*Note:* These phases are explained in greater detail in the following sections.) The rate at which children reach the milestones of language development varies greatly. Although children differ in ability, some generalizations may assist preschool teachers in helping children develop competence in language.

Early Phase (Birth to Three Years)

Before the age of three, children make progress in all of the components of language acquisition: phonology, morphology, syntax, and semantics. (See Chapter Three for an explanation of the components.) One of the most amazing aspects of language development is how accurately children use language at this age. For example, bilingual children may combine elements of one language with those of another. Such language switching is a natural part of dual-language acquisition in bilingual children. (See Chapter Six for a more in-depth look at code switching.)

By age three children have acquired the basic rules of grammar. Although certain forms may still cause problems, the basic elements of grammar have been learned. For example, in English a child might say "goed" for "went" or "mouses" for "mice." Three-year-olds' speech in both languages is generally understandable, although some children may have problems in making certain sounds. In English, consonants in words with several syllables and consonant clusters are especially difficult to pronounce. At this point in development, the bilingual child is able to keep the sounds of both languages separate.

At age three children also understand much spoken language. Some children can understand as many as a thousand words and produce or say several hundred (Hart and Risley 1995). Bilingual children have this capability in two languages, although the total number of words these

children use in one of their languages may be fewer than the number
of words monolingual speakers use in their primary language.

By the age of three, children can respond to what others say, make
requests, issue commands, get attention, and assert their rights. They
may talk to themselves as they play, and language itself may become a
focus of play. Often, they engage in parallel play in which they play
near others but not with them.

Middle Phase (Three to Four Years)

The sound system of both languages is fairly well established when
children reach age four. Pronouncing sounds in English such as "l" and
"r" may still be a problem. "Lizzie" may become "yizzee," and "rabbit"
may be pronounced "wabbit." Other sounds may still give difficulty;
but, increasingly, the child's pronunciation begins to approximate that
of adults.

As bilingual children develop their languages, the length of their
sentences increases. Complex sentences with the conjunctions (connecting words) "and" and "but" begin to appear at this time, as do
phrases in which children express their lack of desire to do something:
"I don't want to!"

At this age children love to ask questions. They begin using "wh"
clauses ("what," "who," "where," "when," and "why"). By age four
children are able to invert auxiliary verbs to form more advanced
questions, such as, "Why did you do that?" Some equivalents to these
English constructions appear in the children's second language, and
some different grammatical structures may develop earlier in the
children's home languages (Escamilla 2000).

Once they have learned how to form questions, the children use
them constantly to test their hypotheses about the world and meanings. A child may ask, "How long do ants live?" The answer, "About a
year," may not mean much to the child, who may then respond,
"Why?" Children are also exploring such concepts as time, quantity,
and relationships. Their vocabulary grows rapidly, but their understanding of words is sometimes quite limited and often literal. When
told, "It is raining cats and dogs," a child may be confused at not
seeing those animals falling from the sky.

Some children will talk aloud to themselves while engaged in play.
This language practice is called *private speech*. It may puzzle some adults
because private speech sometimes sounds like an imaginary conversation. However, private speech is a normal occurrence in the language
development of many children and provides an excellent way for

children to practice and refine their language. As children become older, private speech decreases.

At this age children can engage in effective, appropriate conversation with others and can modify their speech if they are not understood. When they fail to understand what another person says, they often ask for clarification. And when they role-play and use language for dramatic play, they change their speech. They also begin to use polite forms ("May I have some cookies?") and polite formulas ("Thank you" and "Please").

Later Phase (Five to Six Years)

By ages five to six, the bilingual child can use longer and more complex sentences (more than six words) in both languages. Relative clauses appear ("the lady who lives across the street"), as do verbs in the passive voice ("The dog was hit by the car"). Indirect requests ("Can I help?") and comparatives ("This is bigger") also occur.

By age six most children have mastered most of the sounds of their languages. The six-year-old English-speaking child can usually make the difficult "v" and "w" sounds. Second-language learners, however, may find some sounds difficult to pronounce. For example, many native speakers of Spanish encounter difficulties in saying the English "z" of "zip" and the "th" of "thin." The Spanish-speaking child can

usually trill the "r" in Spanish words, such as *rosa* (rose) and *arroz* (rice).

Vocabulary continues to develop in both languages. More multiple meanings of words are understood, and children take words less literally. Thus the statement "Mrs. Tran is a very warm person" is not understood to mean that Mrs. Tran is physically warm. At about this age bilingual children are aware that the meanings of words are arbitrary, an awareness that speakers of a single language develop later in elementary school (Lee 1996).

By age six most children are quite accomplished in their use of language. They can use slang with their peers ("Right on, dude"), show respect when making a request of an adult, and use language to regulate their social status (know which people to address formally). They can adjust their speech to the needs of the listener and know when to add more details to clarify meaning.

Growing appreciation of the multiple meanings of words is reflected in children's humor. Although children's jokes are based mainly on sound plays ("I'm going to the potty" for "party"), puns begin to

4 PRINCIPLES AND PRACTICES

PRINCIPLE

Language development and learning are promoted when preschool teachers and children creatively and interactively use language.

It is essential that children use language to further develop their social and academic English. In addition, through the use of the home language and English, children develop literacy skills that, in turn, enable them to be more competent learners. Teachers should design and implement activities that promote language use as children engage in individual and group activities.

PRACTICES

- Draw children into conversations as much as possible by exploring the meaning of their ideas.

- Be a good listener and promote the children's talk by smiling, nodding, and saying "hmm," "really," and the like.

- Respond to what the children have said by showing that you understand and prompt more speech.

- Encourage children to role-play and engage in extended language activities with one another.

- Let the children talk about their feelings. Model this practice by sharing your feelings with them.

- Model language by playing imitation games in which the child has to do or say what the adult or a puppet says. It is important to speak clearly and to model appropriate language for the children.

- Use puppets and flannel-board stories to encourage children to participate orally.

- Encourage children to bring objects from home that can be described and talked about at school. In this way new vocabulary can be tied to the children's experiences.

- Verbalize what you are doing as you carry out activities. If the activity is repetitious, repeat your verbal description. This approach helps the child link language to the activity.

appear ("If you love candy, why don't you marry it?"). Children at this age find these word plays enormously funny.

Bilingual children can achieve all of these stages in two languages if they have enough exposure and opportunities for use. But, as noted earlier, not all children progress at the same rate. Being encouraged to use language to communicate helps children develop skills. The warmth and responsiveness of preschool teachers can encourage bilingual children to succeed in developing proficiency in speech in each of their languages.

Successive Bilingualism

Successive bilingualism (also known as successive language acquisition, successive second-language acquisition, or sequential bilingualism) applies to children who are learning their second language after their first language has been established. The process of successive bilingualism will be explained in greater detail in Chapter Five.

PRINCIPLES AND PRACTICES

5

PRINCIPLE

Experimenting with the use, form, purpose, and intent of the first and second languages leads to growth in acquiring the second language.

Children love to play with language. When talking to themselves and with others, they experiment with phrases and sounds. Correcting their inaccurate language may hamper their tendency to experiment.

PRACTICES

- Allow trial-and-error speech. Accept mistakes in pronunciation, vocabulary, and grammar. Children should experiment with the sounds of the language just as they do with other components.

- Serve as an English-language model for all children, especially those learning English as a second language. Expand the children's utterances. Repeat with the correct grammar and vocabulary.

- Encourage the children and model ways to elaborate or expand their utterances in the home language and in English. These elaborations can happen during social and instructional conversations, reading activities, or play.

(Continued on next page)

Principle 5 (Continued)

- Celebrate a child's attempts in using a new language. Learning a new language is as difficult for a child as it is for an adult. Children need support. Like adults, they do not enjoy being laughed at when they make mistakes in the new language.

- Point to objects as you name them and coordinate actions with language. Emphasize key words in sentences. Repeat important words in context.

Receptive Bilingualism

If children have few opportunities to speak one of the languages, the result is likely to be *receptive bilingualism,* a term meaning that children understand a great deal more of a language than they can express in words. This experience is probably fairly common for many children. For example, many English learners experience English as the

language of the larger social environment but have few opportunities to use English before they enter preschool. Although their home language may be their dominant language and may continue to be the language of choice, these children will have experienced a great amount of receptive acquisition of English before they enter preschool.

Children who acquire a second language through exposure and not through active use have a different bilingual experience than do children who grow up speaking two languages. The process of receptive bilingualism differs from that of learning a second language after a first language has been established. Although the children are not learning two languages equally because of a strong imbalance favoring the language being used more often, they should not be considered as novices because they are experiencing considerable exposure to the second language.

The point at which children become receptively bilingual is uncertain. In the United States many preschoolers who come from homes in which English is not spoken are exposed to English through television and through older siblings who may be learning English in school and may speak English among themselves. From this exposure children may acquire some English passively but are not considered bilingual.

PRINCIPLES AND PRACTICES

6

PRINCIPLE

Continued use and development of the child's home language will benefit the child as he or she acquires English.

Learning language is an important part of children's cognitive development. One way in which preschool teachers can help children acquire English as a second language is to support the continued development of their home language.

PRACTICES

- *Note:* Preschool teachers who do not speak a child's language can team with family members and other staff who speak that language to establish ways in which the development of the home language can be continued.

- Learn how to say "hello" in each of the languages represented in your classroom. Build this multilingual greeting into arrival or circle time. Teachers can use the same strategy for any other highlighted vocabulary, such as the word of the week or the month. For example: "How do you say *car* in your home language?"

- Share information on the development of first language, second language, and bilingual language with parents and family members throughout the year to ensure that they are aware of what they can do to foster home-language and (when appropriate) second-language development.

- Share information with families about interaction techniques used in the preschool program, such as listening, following the child's lead, expanding the child's utterances, and showing interest and attention.

- Encourage family members to read to each other literature that is valued in their home, including stories of their culture (e.g., parent to child, sibling to other sibling, child to parents, grandparent to child).

- Have English learners and English-speaking children teach each other a few phrases in their home language.

(Continued on next page)

Principle 6 (Continued)

- Point out to the children the many advantages of being able to speak two languages or communicate through more than one system, such as speech and signing.

- Have classroom objects labeled in English and the children's home languages.

Ask Yourself

1. How do I communicate to the children and their families the importance and benefits of learning more than one language?

2. How have I prepared myself to explain the process of both first- and second-language development to families when necessary?

Additional References

Cunningham-Andersson, U., and S. Andersson. 1999. *Growing Up with Two Languages: A Practical Guide.* New York: Routledge.

Knowing Other Languages Brings Opportunities (brochure). N.D. New York: Modern Languages Association. Available by writing to the Office of Foreign Language Programs, Modern Languages Association. flbrochure@mla.org

Zelasko, N., and B. Antunez. 2000. *If Your Child Learns in Two Languages: A Parent's Guide for Improving Educational Opportunities for Children Acquiring English as a Second Language.* Washington, D.C.: National Clearinghouse for English Language Acquisition. Available in English, Spanish, Vietnamese, Chinese, and Haitian Creole at http://www.ncela.gwu.edu/pubs/parent; by telephone at 1-800-321-6223; by fax at 1-800-531-9347; or by e-mail at orders@ncela.gwu.edu.

Note: See pages 115–28 for a list of works cited in this publication.

Stages and Strategies in Second-Language Acquisition

Teacher: "Heart, an only child, came to preschool in August fluent in Thai and speaking no English. At first he spent a great deal of time playing alone, running around the room, yelling, covering his ears, and shrugging his shoulders in frustration. As he played, I sat near him and used lots of gestures paired with words. 'You can jump. I can jump.' As we jumped, he sometimes repeated, 'I jump.' By October he would pull me to the book area, take out a book, and show me with gestures that he was drawing a dinosaur. In late January he was building with blocks and said to me as I approached, 'I made a house for you. I have a big house in Thailand. It is up in a tree (using gestures to make a tree). You come see me. OK?' (He puts his hands together like an airplane)."

Stages of Learning a Second Language

What is the experience of children who have learned one language at home and encounter a second language when they enter preschool? In our society the second language is typically English, although in some cases English-speaking children are exposed to Spanish or another language in the classroom. As noted earlier, many children in the United States have had some exposure to English before preschool. This chapter focuses on children who have had little or no exposure to English before entering preschool. They are not categorized as receptive bilingual because they are learning English as a second language more or less from scratch. Generally, children acquiring a second language move through the following four stages, the names of some stages having been modified to reflect current thinking (Tabors and Snow 1994).

In the first stage children may attempt to use the home language to communicate with others who are speaking a different or second language. In the second stage many pass through a period of observation and listening. They next use telegraphic and formulaic speech in the new or second language and finally begin to use the second language with more fluency.

Not all children go through all stages, and the same children very often weave in and out of each stage, depending on the situation. As a result it may be difficult to characterize where a child is at any particular point. Teachers will want to note the child's language skills through his or her performance in a variety of activities and conversations with many partners throughout the week. Using what that information reveals and what the child's family knows about the child's ability to communicate, the teacher may be able to develop a more accurate informal assessment of the child's language development in both the first and second languages.

Home Language Use

Observational and Listening Period

Telegraphic and Formulaic Speech

Fluid Language Use

The Use of the Home Language to Communicate

Imagine yourself as a young child facing a situation in which many people are speaking a different language. If you want to interact with other children, you can do one of two things—stop talking altogether and use nonverbal ways to communicate or use your home language, which may not be understood by the other children or adults. Some

children opt to use their home language because it has been their only means of communication. In a study Saville-Troike (1989) noticed that children in a child-care setting continued speaking their home language to communicate with other children, who would in turn reply in their own language. This form of communication was generally effective when the children were playing. Communication broke down when the context did not supply enough information or offer enough environmental cues for meaning to be understood. Eventually, of course, children abandon using their home language with those who do not understand it.

The Observational and Listening Period

Previously, this stage was referred to as the silent or nonverbal period because children tend to be quiet when engaged in challenging school activities. However, what children are typically doing at this stage is spending most of their energy listening to make sense of their new language and observing the gestures and environmental cues associated with the new language.

During this phase children may prefer to use other means (gestures, facial expressions, sounds) to communicate rather than talk (speak) to their teachers. Most children spend only a month or two at this stage. However, it can take up to six months, as noted by Hakuta (1974) in his observations of a Japanese girl attending kindergarten in the United States who did not speak for six months.

" **TEACHER**

I was worried because Sandy and Henry were not saying much even though they had been in my class for six months. Then I noticed they were really attending as if to catch every single word that came out of my mouth. I suddenly realized they were processing what they were hearing, getting used to the new sounds in English that were not there in Vietnamese or Mandarin, watching where I was pointing to see what I was labeling. It was soon after that they both started expressing themselves more in English. "

Although children may not be talking at school during this stage, they are attending to and processing language. Like infants learning to speak their first language, second-language learners develop their understanding of the language before they are able to use it to communicate. In more informal situations they will still use their home language and whatever they know of their second language. During this stage children begin actively to crack the code of the second language.

Children rehearse the second language by repeating in a low voice what other speakers say and by playing with the sounds of the new language (Saville-Troike 1989). Repetition seems to be an important part of this rehearsal process. Typically, young children repeat the ends of utterances they hear around them. At this stage their speech is private and not meant as communication but as practice. They seem to be connecting English words with appropriate objects, actions, and situations. Like other young children acquiring their first language, children learning a second language play with the sounds of the language and gradually decipher the sounds, meanings, and patterns of the new one.

Telegraphic and Formulaic Speech

The next stage of second-language acquisition involves trying out the second language—using what is known to communicate. Because children know so little at this point, they typically resort to the use of telegraphic speech and formulas. *Telegraphic speech* refers to the use of a few content words without functional words or certain grammatcal markers that communicate, for example, action, possession, or location. Young children do the same in acquiring the first language. "Mommy milk," "Daddy shoe," and "fish water" are examples. Learning a second language often starts with the use of single words or two-word utterances to name objects: "car," "apple juice," "sandbox." Children are beginning to develop a vocabulary of object names to use in interacting with native speakers.

Formulaic speech, or the use of formulas, is another strategy used by English learners observed by researchers (McLaughlin 1984; Tabors 1997). The formulas are chunks or phrases of language that children use without completely understanding their function. Children use these phrases in certain situations to achieve certain aims because they have heard other children using the phrases successfully (Wong Fillmore 1991). Wong Fillmore's analysis of the children's use of formulaic expressions indicates that the children were using chunks of language to engage in activities that promote language learning. That is, the children were guessing about the conditions under which particular utterances might appropriately be made. By using the formulas and receiving feedback telling them whether their guesses were right or wrong, they were able to test their conclusions. Formulas provided the tools for the children to learn more about their language.

Examples of formulas or formulaic speech:

"I like ____."	"Gimme (Give me) ____."	"I want/wanna ____."
"I like milk."	"Gimme book."	"I want/wanna play."
"I like Bob."	"Gimme juice."	"I want/wanna go."
"I like mommy."	"Gimme blocks."	"I want/wanna doll."

Children involved in this process may seem to be regressing in their ability to use language. The packaged formulas they use are typically grammatically correct, but the children now may be making grammatical errors. The process is similar to the one the child learning English as a first language goes through in learning rules for plurals and past tenses. For example, children may say "runned" instead of "ran." They are no longer using memorized forms but instead are moving to a higher level of language learning by analyzing the language and trying to make sense of it.

Being young scientists, children make hypotheses about language forms and their use in specific situations. Because they are continually testing their hypotheses, they should be provided with rich language environments that foster spoken language (oral communication or talk). Teachers should realize that most of the children's early attempts with language do not involve grammatical errors made intentionally but rather constitute developmental phases of language learning. Consequently, correcting children's speech at the sound of a perceived "error" might have negative consequences on the children's self-esteem and impede the natural developmental process.

> **TEACHER**
>
> I realized how important it was to allow children to use formulas and expressions that they have learned, even when their use was not always correct. When children used such expressions as 'How you do dese bananas?' or 'Gimme that thing,' I recognized they were interacting verbally and that this was more important than my need for grammatical correctness.

Fluid Language Use

As children demonstrate an understanding of the rules of English, they are able to apply them to achieve increasing control over the language. At this point they are using the new language much more creatively and begin to sound more like native speakers. The types of English used by children at this stage are referred to as (1) social English; and (2) academic English.

Social English, a variety of English used first by children during this phase of language development, refers to the use by children of more fluid speech (language) in the second language. Considered to be informal and predominantly spoken, it is characterized by short and simple sentence structures and, therefore, requires a smaller vocabulary than does academic English (Cummins 1981). Social English is sometimes referred to by educators as conversational English (Shefelbine 1998).

Children use social English most often in interactions with friends and adults in relaxed or playful situations. Some children may progress in this stage with incredible speed. Others may take noticeably longer to use their new language in social contexts, causing some teachers to be concerned about the children's lower progress. By drawing on their knowledge of early childhood development, those teachers should remember that children reach developmental milestones, including those in first-language and second-language development, at different rates. That knowledge will help teachers view the progress of the children with accurate perspective.

Although children may feel comfortable in communicating with others in social situations, they may not be ready to participate effectively in more cognitively demanding situations (Cummins and Swain 1986). Children who use social English to greet their teachers in the playground or during mealtimes may mislead their teachers into thinking that the children can participate fully in all learning activities.

Academic English, in contrast to social English, takes much longer to learn. Studies have shown that school-age children require five to seven years to master academic English (Thomas and Collier 2002). Academic English, more formal than social English, requires the use of longer, more complex sentence structures. Children also need to master a larger vocabulary (Cummins 1981). Academic English requires children to perform in all four of the language skills addressed in school: listening, speaking, reading, and writing. Because of the advanced requirements of academic English and the time it takes to master it, the use of a child's home language as the child masters English will help the child learn important concepts. Some teachers who are not proficient in a child's home language provide academic support in that language by planning activities to be implemented by family or community volunteers who speak the language. When no adults in the classroom speak a child's home language, the teacher can use other strategies included in this guide, such as the following, many of which are common strategies used by preschool teachers to make concepts meaningful for children.

Strategies in Second-Language Acquisition

A number of cognitive and social strategies are used by young second-language learners (Wong Fillmore 1990; Tabors 1997):

Cognitive strategies used by children	Teaching tips to match the strategies
Assume that what people are saying is directly relevant to the situation at hand or to what they or you are experiencing.	*Make sure that your speech matches what you are referring to.* If you hold up a paper pumpkin but talk about Thanksgiving, a child may think the label for the pumpkin is Thanksgiving.
Learn and use some expressions you understand. "I want ____ (juice, toy, play, and so on)." "_____ please."	*Use speech and phrases that are predictable and repetitive.* "Let's ____ (read, play, clean up, etc.)." "It's time to ____ (eat, sleep, go home)."
Make the most of the language you have. A child may learn the word "dog" and use that as a general label until he or she learns more refined descriptive words, such as "puppy," "terrier," or "Spot."	*Accept the label that the child uses and model the new descriptor for him or her.* "I see the dog too. His name is Spot."
Work on the big things; save the details for later. Many preschool English learners will leave out articles, adjectives, and even verbs as they are mastering English. Yes/No___. ("Yes book" for "I'd like to read." "No food" for "I'm not hungry.")	*Serve as a total language model. Refrain from correcting children in their attempts to communicate in their new language since such corrections might cause them embarrassment.* Child: "I no want chip potato." Teacher: "All right. You are done with your potato chips."

Social strategies used by children	Teaching tips to match the strategies
Join a group and act as though you understand what is going on, even if you do not. The child may nod as a way to participate in the conversation or repeat a word a peer said.	*When children are engaged in cooperative learning or play, serve as an interpreter for both the fluent English speaker and the child learning English.* "Sara is building a tunnel. You like to play with Sara. You pushed your car through the tunnel."
Give the impression, with a few well-chosen words, that you can speak the language. Some children pick up on a popular character, fast-food chain, or theme and refer to it as a way to make friends.	*Acknowledge the child's attempt to join a conversation and model more advanced language by extending his or her one or two words into more complete sentences.* "Yes, SuperBurgers sells hamburgers. We're eating hamburgers for lunch."
Count on your friends for help. Young English learners will sit next to or play with a peer who accepts the way they talk or stay quiet and includes them in the activity in natural ways.	*Strategically pair children with helpful peers who can serve as good language and interactive models.* Acknowledge the peer's friendly actions and responses.

Some children who acquire a second language quite rapidly apply such strategies in particular social situations. For example, they seek out children who speak the language they want to learn and engage in verbally challenging play, such as dramatic play. They eagerly use what they know in order to communicate.

Children benefit significantly from the guidance and assistance of adults and other more capable peers while engaged in meaningful, culturally relevant activities. The preschool environment is ideally suited for developing first and second languages because language is used in concrete, conversational, and meaningful interactions.

Another way to present the various strategies that a teacher can use to support second-language learners is presented in the following "Research to Practice." These strategies relate to the different stages involved in learning a second language and will support all children as they progress in their language development. Some particularly crucial strategies to offer to children at specific stages of their second-language acquisition are indicated by the checkmarks. An important point to keep in mind is that a child may move into and out of these different

(*Continued on page 56*)

RESEARCH TO PRACTICE

Strategies for Responding to Stages of Communication That Children Move Into and Out of as They Learn a Second Language

Teacher support strategy	Stage of learning a second language			
	Home language	Observational/ listening	Telegraphic and formulaic	Fluid use of second language
Start with what the child knows: Use a few words in the child's home language (come, bathroom, eat) to allow for low-level communication.	✔	✔		
Start slowly: Allow the child to become familiar with the classroom situation before approaching him or her with questions and directives in English.	✔	✔		
Use scaffold communication: Combine words with some type of gesture, action, or directed gaze.	✔	✔	✔	✔
Provide safe havens: Allow the child to regain energy and focus by providing spaces and activities in which the child can participate with few, if any, expectations for verbal communication.	✔	✔	✔	✔
Get help from the English-speaking children: Show the child's peers ways to communicate and ask questions in order to encourage interaction and provide additional language models.	✔	✔	✔	✔

Research to Practice (Continued)

Teacher support strategy	Stage of learning a second language			
	Home language	Observational/ listening	Telegraphic and formulaic	Fluid use of second language
Expand and extend: Start with what the child already knows and expand on his or her language. If the child says "car," the teacher can reply, "That is a red car."			✔	✔
Raise expectations: Request an oral response from the child rather than only a gesture when he or she shows signs of readiness to talk.			✔	✔
Use repetition: Say the same thing more than once to give the child an opportunity to understand what is being said.	✔	✔	✔	✔
Talk about the here and now: Refer to the present situation to allow the child to understand the context of communication.	✔	✔	✔	✔
Do fine tuning: Restate the message in a form that the child can understand when he or she at first seems not to understand.	✔	✔	✔	✔
Offer consistent routines: Help the child learn quickly where to go and what to expect so that he or she can become a member of the group.	✔	✔	✔	✔
Ensure inclusion: Use the child's name to invite him or her to participate in small-group activities.	✔	✔	✔	✔

Source: Adapted from Tabors (1997), chapters 4, 5, and 6.

stages, depending on the content being discussed and the context in which it is presented.

For example, when a teacher talks about farm animals, the child may have few context cues to assist in comprehension and may be functioning at the observational and listening stage in this situation. Or when the child is looking at farm animals depicted as a cartoon or in an abstract art drawing, the child may have difficulty recognizing the animal and labeling it. But, while on a field trip to the farm, more context cues might enhance the child's communication. These cues might include the sight of real animals, the smell of the farm, the noises made by the farm animals, and the farmer's talking in the child's home language. At the farm a child's communication may sound more telegraphic or even fluid. Therefore, teachers should tailor the type of supportive strategies they use to fit each lesson or activity.

Ask Yourself

1. How can I provide opportunities for the children in my class to practice their new language or use their home language when they are playing outside the classroom, in the pretend play area, or in other activity centers?

2. What is the level of my awareness of each child's temperament? How can I respect each child's preferred style of interaction, especially as he or she is acquiring a second language?

3. What community resources can I use to provide language models for students in my class whose home language I do not speak?

Additional References

Developing the Young Bilingual Learner. 1998. Washington, D.C.: National Association for the Education of Young Children and Resources and Instruction in Staff Excellence. Videotape.

Lightbown, P., and N. Spada. 1999. *How Languages Are Learned* (Second edition). New York: Oxford University Press.

Meier, D. 2004. *The Young Child's Memory for Words: Developing First and Second Language and Literacy.* New York: Teachers College Press.

Note: See pages 115–28 for a list of works cited in this publication.

6

Code Switching and Language Loss

Parent: "Angelica has three older siblings who are bilingual, and all of them have no problems in speaking, reading, and writing either Spanish or English. So my husband and I have decided to continue speaking to Angelica in Spanish at home while her teacher uses English with her at school."

Code Switching

Parents and teachers of young bilingual children often notice that young English learners mix languages, a practice referred to in this guide as code switching. *Code switching* can be defined as the use of two or more languages in the same stream of talk or as the ability to alternate between two language systems in a conversation (Pérez and Torres-Guzmán 1996). It is often used by young children exposed to more than one language. While it may be tempting to see code switching as a problem, learning two languages simultaneously does not appear to interfere with learning either one (Ashworth and Wakefield 2004; Gass and Selinker 2001). Researchers have found that code switching is not just an early strategy in the development of a second language, but it can also serve many other purposes for bilingual children. Furthermore, by three years of age most children will have learned to distinguish the languages to which they are exposed and use each language in different social situations or environments appropriately (Berk 2003).

Examples of code switching are common in the literature on bilingual children. Leopold (1949) observed a bilingual child, Hildegard, who spoke English with her mother and German with her father. Examples of Hildegard's mixing languages follow:

"*Die Milch* pour*en*" ("Pour the milk").

"*Musik* practic*en*" ("Practice music").

"*Ich habe ge*yawn*t*" ("I yawned").

"For two month*e*" ("For two months").

Similarly, McClure (1977) and Genishi (1981) describe how in their studies bilingual Mexican American preschool children expertly blended speech:

"I put the fork *en la mesa*" ("on the table").

"*Yo quiero ir* outside" ("I want to go").

The previous examples show that, even when children mix their two languages, they tend to honor the grammatical rules of each. As they speak the new language, they attempt to honor the phonological rules of each language as well (Zentella 1997). These skills show how advanced the language skills of young bilingual children truly are.

Studies have shown that, as early as three years of age (Gregory 1997; Fantini 1985; McClure 1977), children can switch languages to address individuals in appropriate language to serve their own social goals, such as to emphasize a point, honor the language preference of their listener, please adults, elaborate, clarify, interrupt, change a topic, and be included or exclude other children as they negotiate new roles in social situations.

These examples of code switching indicate preschool children's increasing proficiency not only in using language but also in participating in a variety of social and cultural contexts (Pérez and Torres-Guzmán 1996). Many of the children demonstrate competence in controlling when, where, and with whom they switch.

Teachers also switch codes when speaking to bilingual children and their families in an attempt to navigate between two languages. At times, especially when a word or concept does not exist in one of the

7

PRINCIPLES AND PRACTICES

PRINCIPLE

Code switching is a normal part of language development for many bilingual children.

Code switching is a common practice in bilingual families and communities. As a result, children are following the language practices around them when they engage in code switching.

PRACTICES

- Recognize that code switching is a natural process for bilingual children. At times they use this strategy to communicate when the necessary vocabulary in a language is lacking. They are also learning a sophisticated way of using language.

- Value code switching as you would other experiments with language. As children get older, switching languages represents a complex accomplishment in language reflecting a knowledge of an advanced system of rules.

- Avoid side-by-side translations. Some programs assign one teacher to use the child's home language and another teacher to use English. A teacher can serve as a language model in the language he or she knows well.

- Use code switching carefully to ensure that all of your students understand what is being said.

- Read and make available to your students bilingual children's books that provide written examples of code switching.

- Discuss with families their concerns about code switching and its merits.

languages, teachers will insert a word from a different language as they speak to illustrate a particular concept. Under those circumstances code switching can be considered an acceptable practice for teachers (Faltis 1989; Jacobson 1990; Romero and Parrino 1994).

Language Loss

Children rarely have both languages in balance. Typically, one language is stronger in use and exposure. When such dominance occurs, the elements of the weaker language can quickly be lost. Children may forget vocabulary and even rules of grammar. Many bilingual children lose much of their first language as they go through the U.S. school system and their exposure to English increases. Even when

parents continue to use the first language with their children, it may not develop to the same degree that the second language does.

During the process of losing a first language, children may appear to have limited proficiency in both languages. Most likely, they are undergoing a developmental phase during which the lack of use of the first

language results in a decline in proficiency while the knowledge of the second language is not yet at an age-appropriate level. In time most children attain age-appropriate levels in the second language, although they may retain an accent and transfer elements of their first language that mark them as nonnative speakers.

Preschool teachers need to be aware that this phase of language development is temporary. Even though a bilingual child's performance in either language appears to lag behind that of monolingual speakers, the child may possess a total or combined vocabulary and language skills exceeding those of monolingual speakers. What appear to be deficiencies in both languages should be more appropriately understood as language imbalance. At certain points in the development of their languages, bilingual children do not perform as well as native speakers do in either language. Eventually, however, most

PARENT

" I spoke only Spanish until I started school. I can't remember exactly when it happened, but eventually I lost most of it. I can communicate with my parents, I understand what they're saying, but I often have trouble finding the right words to answer them. Sometimes they even laugh at my attempts. That's why I don't want Breanna to lose the Spanish she learned and used when she was staying with my parents. I want her to keep her home language. I'm glad you use both English and Spanish in the classroom. "

bilingual children are able to reach age-level proficiency in their dominant language, given enough exposure and opportunities to use that language. The age at which a child reaches this more balanced level of bilingualism depends on a variety of factors, such as the age at which that child began acquisition of each language, the quality and quantity of exposure to each of those languages, and the social climate surrounding the use of those languages (Ovando and Collier 1998). As a result the age at which the abilities of English learning become similar to those of their monolingual peers will vary.

A language can be maintained only through exposure to speakers of that language and opportunities to use it. For many young children a significant reduction in use of the home language leads to its loss. Therefore, families need to be encouraged to provide sufficient opportunities for children to speak their home language so that it can be maintained. Some families enroll their child in after-school or weekend language classes, which can support the development of the home language and connect the child to the culture associated with that language community. Such options are not available in all communities or may be too expensive for many immigrant families. Additional examples of how to provide these opportunities are provided under Principle 6 in Chapter Four.

When children are older, many regret having lost proficiency in their first language. If older children and adolescents cannot communicate well with their parents or grandparents, the cost to the family can be great (in the loss of communication and of respect for the parents and relatives who speak the home language). Preschool teachers should work with parents, family members, and staff proficient in the child's home language to provide ample opportunities to foster the child's language development in the home language while the child is acquiring English.

Ask Yourself

1. How can I make sure that the children have plenty of opportunities to engage in conversation with both peers and adults so that their language development will flourish?

2. How can I balance the amount of talking I do in order to allow the children to participate more through their own use of language?

Additional References

Brice, A., and L. Rosa-Lugo. 2000. "Code Switching: A Bridge or Barrier Between Two Languages?" *Multiple Voices for Ethnically Diverse Exceptional Learners,* Vol. 4, No. 1, 1–12.

Peyton, J., and others, editors. 2001. *Heritage Languages in America: Preserving a National Resource.* Washington D.C.: Delta Systems and the Center for Applied Linguistics.

Wong Fillmore, L. 2000. "Loss of Family Languages: Should Educators Be Concerned?" *Theory into Practice,* Vol. 39, No. 4, 203–10.

Note: See pages 115–28 for a list of works cited in this publication.

English Learners with Disabilities or Other Special Needs

At a recent early childhood conference, teachers raised the following questions: "How do I know if a child is experiencing difficulties in learning alanguage, such as a speech disorder, or is just going through the process of second-language acquisition?" "Is it OK for me to use English and the child's home language at school when the child has a disability?" "How long should I wait before I make a referral to special education for a child who is learning English as a second language?"

A Language Disorder Versus a Language Difference

Early childhood teachers ask questions similar to the preceding ones when working with young children who are English learners and may or may not have a disability or other special needs. Although the answers to such questions may not always come easily or clearly, the teacher should collaborate with the child's family and available specialists to determine the existence of an authentic language disorder rather than a language difference. A *language disorder* is "an inability to understand and process language either expressively or receptively" (Tompkins 2002, 6). A child who speaks another language or a variety of a standard language is said to have a *language difference* (Hirsh-Pasek, Kochanoff, and Newcombe 2005). Working with family members

RESEARCH TO PRACTICE

Behaviors Demonstrated by English Learners and Children with Disabilities

English learners may exhibit certain classroom behaviors that concern their teachers and may cause the teachers to refer the learners to special education classes. Although those behaviors are similar to those exhibited by children with disabilities, the reasons for their existence are different. For English learners the behaviors are temporary adjustments in response to being placed in an environment in which they fail to understand the rules or the language being spoken. Therefore, teachers should team up with professionals knowledgeable about second-language acquisition to sort out which behaviors are due to learning English as a second language and which are due to other causes. Behaviors that can be misinterpreted include the following:

- Speaks infrequently
- Speaks excessively (in the home language or in English)
- Refuses to answer questions
- Confuses similar sounding words
- Is unable to tell or retell stories
- Has poor recall
- Uses poor pronunciation
- Uses poor syntax and grammar
- Does not volunteer information

Adapted from Ortiz and Maldonado-Colon (1986).

and specialists as a team will help teachers determine which languages and communication systems will best support the overall learning and development for a particular child.

Because a shortage of trained bilingual and bicultural staff exists in early childhood special education, inexperienced educators and specialists involved in evaluating and educating culturally and linguistically diverse young children may judge various approaches to learning, knowledge bases, behaviors, and, of course, language skills as being deficient rather than merely different.

Another reason for early childhood educators, parents, and administrators to proceed cautiously when trying to distinguish a language disorder from a language difference is the effect of the learning context (Gutiérrez-Clellen and Peña 2001). If most children in the educational and care setting are progressing according to state, local, and cultural norms, then the children's low achievement in language could be attributed to a failure to respond to adequate, age-appropriate instruction. However, if a significant percentage of the children are showing delays in learning, the instruction or care may be inadequate. In that case larger, more comprehensive programmatic and staffing issues should be examined (Corson 2001). Similarly, if children are not responding to a particular form of assistance, a reorganization of the learning activity to include other forms of scaffolding or assisted learning may be required. Before referral and diagnosis occur, therefore, environmental, attitudinal, philosophical, and staffing adjustments should be made.

Special Education Programs and English Learners

Some young English learners have been placed in programs for children with disabilities because of a shortage of available and affordable preschool programs in the community or the belief that individualized instruction would be helpful. Although this practice is well intentioned, evidence shows that it may harm children more than help them. Wilkinson and Ortiz (1986) found that after three years spent in special programs for students with learning disabilities, English learners were further behind than when they were initially placed in those programs.

The most recent reauthorization of the Individuals with Disabilities Education Act (IDEA) stipulates that children should not be found

RESEARCH HIGHLIGHTS

A mistaken belief exists that young children learning more than one language will have delayed language acquisition. This notion holds that when a child is acquiring two languages at the same time, the onset of the first words is delayed, and the rate of vocabulary growth lags behind that of speakers of a single language. Even researchers who report this finding are quick to point out that if both languages are taken into account, bilingual children have a vocabulary that exceeds that of the monolingual child. Goodz (1994) reported no delay in the onset of the first words in a sampling of bilingual children. Furthermore, in at least one of their languages, the children had developed as much vocabulary as had monolingual children of the same age. It seems clear, therefore, that the belief that the children are delayed during this process may often be an incorrect assumption.

In their studies on the language development of children with Down syndrome, Mundy and others (1995) found that when teachers and parents took into account the children's skills in English, the home language, and sign language, they realized that the children were at or above the same level in vocabulary and syntax as monolingual children of the same age who had Down syndrome.

eligible for special education services if their learning challenges are primarily the result of environmental, cultural, or economic disadvantage. Consequently, teachers and specialists must ensure that young children are assessed in their home language(s). Assessment results should also reflect the family's knowledge of their children's development, abilities, and learning challenges when eligibility for services is being determined and an individualized family service plan (IFSP) or individualized education program (IEP) is being developed.

All the principles and practices listed in this guide apply to young English learners with disabilities. Research has shown that children with disabilities can learn more than one language and can function bilingually as effectively as their typically developing peers (Candelaria-Greene 1996; Miles 1996). Their delays in communication manifest their cognitive, motor, and social delays and are not associated with their growing up bilingually. The language delays in both languages coexist with their disabilities, but bilingualism is not the cause of their delays (Baker 2000a).

Sometimes teachers and specialists mistakenly assume that a child with a disability will be confused by being exposed to more than one language, particularly because the child already has a disability. As a result they recommend that only one language be used to communicate with that child, and English is often the language of choice. Such a recommendation can adversely affect the learning and social development of the child and his or her family.

Several factors come into play for a bilingual child with a disability who is exposed to only one language when that language is not the home language. First, by suddenly being placed in an all-English context, the child has little recourse to draw on what is familiar, comfortable, and reassuring in communication and social interactions. Second, the child will have to spend much of his or her energy and concentration on learning a second language while struggling with other learning challenges. Third, although the child may, over time, start to understand and use English, the child may lose the ability to benefit from the critical support and guidance provided by the family in the home language because his or her home language is not also being nurtured.

When language and communication goals are developed for monolingual children with cerebral palsy, Down syndrome, or autism, the children's communication abilities are considered in comparison with those of other children with the same diagnosis and degree of delay.

During an informal conference with the mother of a 4-year-old child with autism:

TEACHER
In the classroom Samuel speaks to me in English and to the classroom assistant in Spanish. Does he use both languages at home?

PARENT
Yes, since he began talking, he uses English with me and with his brothers, and he uses Spanish with his father. Sometimes he'll substitute Spanish words when he doesn't know the English, like I don't think he knows the word 'slipper,' so he always uses 'chancleta.' But he easily switches back and forth between languages.

Similarly, bilingual children with disabilities benefit from having their communication abilities compared with those of other children with the same diagnosis and degree of delay as language and communication goals are explored and developed for them.

Coordinating Language and Communication Goals

A critical need exists to establish a system of coordination among the adults caring for and working with the young bilingual child with disabilities. Such a system will provide a clear idea as to what language(s) and modes of communication have been identified as

appropriate for learning and social interaction. This shared understanding comes only from the collaboration of special educators, early childhood educators, and bilingual educators with the child's family. Both teachers and administrators must be involved.

The collaborative team needs to consider how each spoken language and augmentative communication system, such as sign language or a picture-symbol system, will be used during the

(Continued on page 70)

RESEARCH HIGHLIGHTS

Deaf and Hard-of-Hearing Children from Spanish-Speaking Homes

Gerner de Garcia (1995a, 1995b) found that for students who already had a foundation in Spanish as their home language and signing, a trilingual approach of using Spanish and American Sign Language while spoken English was being introduced was successful for Spanish-dominant deaf and hard-of-hearing students. He also found that some immigrant deaf and hard-of-hearing students arrive in U.S. schools underschooled and may, therefore, not know any sign language or written or spoken language. So they would be in a position to acquire two language forms—spoken English and some form of sign language.

PRINCIPLES AND PRACTICES

8

PRINCIPLE

Coordination and collaboration among families, teachers, and specialists become crucial in supporting the language and literacy development of children with disabilities and other special needs.

Communication between teachers and families is crucial in serving all children more effectively, especially when children have unique needs. In such cases coordination and collaboration between teachers and families are necessary supports for the child.

PRACTICES

- Determine with the family what their language use and preferences are. Develop a plan to support the family's goals while addressing goals for the classroom and for IFSP and IEP language.

- Vary and adapt the amount of adult guidance according to children's abilities so that each child is in charge of his or her own learning as much as possible.

- Connect learning goals and activities with local and state curriculum and standards.

- Use all the senses (vision, hearing, touch, taste) when introducing and presenting vocabulary and other concepts.

- Provide multiple opportunities for children with disabilities to interact with their peers in English and their home language.

- Model for students ways to interact with and assist classmates who have disabilities.

- Use physical gestures, signed words, visual cues, and props when the actual item is not an option (or pair the actual item with one or more of the cues) to promote successful communication in English and the children's home languages.

- Implement the use of technology (e.g., computers, voice output devices, switch-operated toys) throughout the classroom as another means of supporting student learning.

- Offer adapted or specialized materials (e.g., recorded books, Braille books and other printed material, large and bold print, adapted handles on various materials) throughout the classroom to enhance active participation.

- Make appropriate environmental changes (e.g., color contrast in materials, good lighting, reduced noise level, comfortable seating, and work spaces) to support children's learning.

course of the child's day. Any system or combination of communication systems will have optimal results when implemented in a natural, and nonstressful manner. The IFSP or IEP should, therefore, specify which instructional goals and objectives will be delivered in the native language, which will be delivered in English, and, if applicable, which will be delivered in an alternative mode of communication appropriate for English learners (Artiles and Ortiz 2002).

Ask Yourself

1. What access do I have to colleagues who are knowledgeable about second-language acquisition and can help me sort out whether a student is demonstrating a language difference or a language disorder?

2. How frequently do I meet with every team member for each child in my class who has either an IFSP or an IEP?

3. How prepared and comfortable am I in using the different communication systems that the children in my class bring in from other settings? If necessary, where do I go to get support?

4. What can I do to provide an inclusive setting for the children with disabilities in my class so that they have access to and benefit from the many language and literacy activities I offer the rest of my students?

Additional References

Klein, M. D., and D. Chen. 2001. *Working with Children from Diverse Cultural Backgrounds.* Albany, N.Y.: Delmar.

Lynch, E. W., and M. J. Hanson. 1998. *Developing Cross-cultural Competence: A Guide for Working with Young Children and Their Families* (Second edition). Baltimore: Paul H. Brookes.

Roseberry-McKibbin, C. 2003. *Assessment of Bilingual Learners: Language Difference or Disorder?* Rockville, Md.: American Speech-Language-Hearing Association.

Note: See pages 115–28 for a list of works cited in this publication.

Recommended
Early Literacy Practices

Teacher: "Andres speaks Russian. No one on the staff speaks this language. His mother stayed for several hours on the first day to show Andres around the center and to explain the daily routine. I use a picture schedule so he knows what to expect throughout the day, a wide variety of props, and books with lots of pictures and gesturing, such as patting the chair where he can sit as I say, 'Sit on the chair.' I've shared these strategies with the other children in my classroom, and they are helping him with the same techniques."

Defining Early Literacy

Early literacy has been defined in many ways, and each definition has implications for teaching and guiding children's development. Koralek and Collins (1997, 10) state that early "literacy describes the gradual, ongoing process of learning to understand and use language that begins at birth and continues through the early childhood years. During this period children first learn to use oral forms of language—listening and speaking—and then begin to explore and make sense of written forms—reading and writing."

Research on brain development has revealed the importance of early relationships and healthy social-emotional and language development. That research will ordinarily inform early literacy planning and instruction conducted by teachers and programs (Snow, Burns, and Griffin 1998). Koralek and Collins (1997) point out that providing children many opportunities to listen and speak gives the children an important foundation for reading and writing. Children who are read to often are exposed to the joy of reading. Even with these opportunities with language and literacy, about eight to ten percent of the children still encounter difficulties with learning to read (Snow, Burns, and Griffin 1998). Most children come into the world ready to learn spoken language but will need carefully planned instruction to learn to read or make sense of written language (Berg and Stegelman 2003; Kaderavek and Justice 2004).

Two components of early literacy are knowing how to construct meaning through reading and through writing. "Reading and writing are always situated within *discourse communities*—groups of people with socially and culturally determined language practices, behaviors, and ways of thinking about the world" (Owocki 2001, 6). Therefore, a third related component of literacy development is the knowledge that children need to negotiate reading and writing within their communities. Therefore, children and their families should be seen as contributors to their literacy development and practices just as for their oral communication practices. The benefits of creating positive and meaningful language and literacy experiences in English and the home language for young bilingual children are far-reaching. As Snow, Burns, and Griffin (1998, 324–25) state: ". . . Being biliterate, or having the ability to read and write in two languages, confers numerous intellectual, cultural, economic, and social benefits."

Connecting Home and School Literacy Practices

Duke and Purcell-Gates (2003) emphasize the importance of tapping into the literacy practices used at home as a resource and bridge to presenting literacy practices used at school. Often, teachers ask parents and family members to use school vocabulary and literacy practices at home. But they may forget to do the reverse (i.e., to bring

PRINCIPLE

Engaging in multiple literacy practices, such as reading books, singing songs, and reciting poetry, is part of the daily life of many families.

Preschool teachers should recognize and capitalize on the richness of language use in children's families. For example, poetry has been found to play an important role in the language development of some Korean American families (Scarcella 1990). By gathering the following information, a teacher will be better able to tap into the literacy practices and knowledge base the children are already familiar with and use that information as a resource in the classroom.

PRACTICES

Ask parents about the ways they engage in the use of language and literacy at home:

- Do they read to their children? If so, what kinds of printed materials do the adults and children in the home select?

  Mail, letters
  Newspapers
  Popular magazines
  Religious books and written materials
  Cookbooks and food labels
  School newsletters and information flyers
  Children's story books
  Folktales
  Nursery rhymes
  Poetry
  Letters or cards from relatives
  Television guides
  Board games
  Children's coloring or activity books

- Do they recite rhymes?

(Continued on next page)

Principle 9 (Continued)

- Do they tell stories about relatives and friends?
- Do they sing along to music? If so, what type of music? Does the child have certain favorite songs?
- Do they tell folktales?
- Do they play word games?
- Do they share proverbs?
- Do they repeat limericks?
- Do they have family conversations?

  When do your best conversations happen?
  What does your child like to talk about?
  What do you like to talk about?

into the classroom or care setting the richness of literacy practices, tools, and materials that already exist at home).

The recent focus on the importance of early literacy is leading early childhood educators to seek guidance as they attempt both to respect children's home language and culture and to introduce academic English. Research has shown that children can transfer language and literacy skills from one language to another (Durgunoglu and Öney 2000; Jiménez, Garcia, and Pearson 1995; Lanauze and Snow 1989). When the children's home languages have the same writing conventions as those for English (for example, one reads from left to right and top to bottom), the children will most likely apply those principles to reading in the second language. The stronger the children's language and literacy skills are in the home languages, the more likely the children will transfer those skills successfully to their second language. (The foundation provided by the first language for learning a second language was explained in the earlier discussion of the threshold hypothesis in Chapter Four).

For children in kindergarten and the elementary grades, several basic cognitive abilities have been found to transfer across languages and facilitate the process of second-language acquisition and literacy development (Baddeley 1988; Case 1985; Geva and Ryan 1993). The children are able to:

1. Use information from what is being discussed and connect that information with what they already know to make sense of new concepts.

2. Use their knowledge of letter-sound relationships to begin to decode print.

3. Access words and their meanings from memory.

4. Apply their knowledge of word order as they start to read or write.

5. Understand the story or text read to them and ask questions when they are confused or when the reading does not make sense to them.

6. Put their thoughts into writing.

Children can transfer their knowledge of decoding skills and strategies for determining meaning when reading text in a second language. In the task of decoding, the basic linguistic knowledge and cognitive processes involved are letter recognition, phonological awareness, letter-sound relationships (phonics), the blending of sounds to form words, and the matching of print to known words stored in long-term memory. Phonological awareness and decoding ability in Spanish have been found to be related to the ability of bilingual children in grade one to decode texts in English (Durgunoglu, Nagy, and Hancin-Bhatt 1993). Basic cognitive processes involved in sound- and letter-processing skills in Spanish were linked to the decoding of words in English. The positive aspects of transfer in word recognition have been observed even when the child's first language is a nonalphabetic language. For example, a study of bilingual Chinese children in grades one through eight found that the children's ability to detect Chinese rhyme was significantly related to their phonological and decoding skills in English (Gottardo and others 2001).

RESEARCH HIGHLIGHTS

From their review of research on literacy practices of Latino students, Barrera and Jiménez (2002) found that the more effective teachers:

1. Offered a balance between attention to decoding and meaning of text

2. Provided conditions that allowed students to utilize all of their cultural and linguistic knowledge (Some teachers did so by providing students with a summary of a story in Spanish before reading the story aloud in English. Other teachers allowed and encouraged children to employ whichever language was most comfortable rather than English only.)

3. Increased their connection with parents and families by seeking comments and incorporating them into instructional practices when suitable

Teaching Through Language

An important distinction exists between teaching through language and teaching language. For young children, using language in a conversational, engaging manner provides a vehicle for introducing new concepts and reviewing those already learned. Their learning is enhanced when they can make a connection with something familiar. Therefore, the use of their home language and culture, when possible, will help them become emergent readers when they have not yet mastered English (TESOL 2001).

Making a connection with the child's first language should not, however, preclude introducing written text in English to English learners. Many preschool English learners recognize environmental print in English from signs, logos, labels, television programs, and billboards that they enjoy "reading" when seen in written materials at school. Big illustrated books containing rhyme, rhythm, and repetition are also very helpful. A carefully planned literacy curriculum that offers a well-balanced presentation of literacy skills through sequential instruction and dedicated time for children and teachers to engage in reading different types of text represents the type of comprehensive approach to literacy instruction that will benefit young English learners (Torgesen 2002).

Often, the teacher speaks only English or is bilingual but has children in class who speak several different languages. In those instances the teacher should draw on the language skills of paraprofessionals, family members, and community volunteers to support the continued concept development of children not yet fluent in English. In addition, the teacher can implement the many other practices presented in this guide to support children's development in language and literacy.

For some bilingual children the task of learning to read and write in two languages may be more challenging if their languages have different writing systems rather than only different scripts. For example, children learning to read and write in English and Chinese, which have different writing systems, may have a harder time doing so than will children learning to read and write in English and Hebrew, which have different scripts but share an alphabetic writing system (Harding-Esch and Riley 2003).

Reading Books Aloud to English Learners

Reading books aloud to children helps them acquire information and skills, such as the meaning of words, the makeup of a book, a variety of writing styles, facts about their world, differences between conversations and written language, and knowledge of printed letters and words along with the relationship between sound and print (Early Childhood Head Start Task Force 2002). Using different types of books

ensures that the children will find at least a few books that meet their interests and preferences. Storybooks are traditional favorites for many young children. Other children may prefer books that have information about animals, nature, transportation, careers, or travel, for example. Alphabet books, picture dictionaries, and books with diagrams and overlays (such as those about the human body) also catch the interest of children. And some children particularly enjoy books containing poetry, children's songs and verses, or folktales.

Offering different types of books also provides flexibility in choosing one or two languages in which to read a story. Several researchers have stressed the importance of using authentic books or multicultural literature that portrays children and adults of diverse U.S. cultures engaging in genuine family and community activities and communicating in their language (Barrera, Quiroa, and Valdivia 2002; Natheson-Mejía and Escamilla 2003; Schon 1997). *Note:* Avoid books and written materials that reinforce stereotypes and depict people in offensive ways. Other options for the teacher to use are the following:

- Photo albums with captions in English or the home language are an excellent way to draw out even those children who typically do not participate in traditional reading of books. Images of family members, pets, and outings can inspire conversations and lead to shared experiences.

- Picture books serve as outstanding vehicles for the teacher and the child to interpret or make up their own version of the story. In this manner the story can be told in any language or combination of languages.

- English books with words or phrases in the home language are especially useful for engaging groups in which two major language groups are represented in a class. For children already proficient in English, the books introduce vocabulary in their peers' native language. For children whose native language is still dominant, the books help them understand at least parts of a story and stay engaged in the reading experience. For bilingual children the books can reinforce their dual-language skills, allowing them to see how they can be interpreters or language brokers for those peers who understand only one of the languages. A good example of this type of book for classes with English and Spanish speakers is *Pío Peep: Traditional Spanish Nursery Rhymes* (Ada and Campoy 2003).

- Bilingual books may have English text on one side of a page and a second language on the other side. The English text can be read by a staff person on one occasion, and the non-English text can be read by a family member or a classroom volunteer on another occasion.

- Some teachers make versions of the same book available in English and in one or more languages. This practice allows children to compare and contrast vocabulary and writing conventions in different languages and for adults in the classroom to read to the children in their stronger language. It also demonstrates the teacher's valuing of a multilingual and multicultural learning environment.

- Child-generated texts or stories that children dictate to their teachers are very meaningful to all children, including English learners, because these stories reflect experiences that are familiar to the children. In addition, "writing" their own phrases and stories provides young children with a concrete way to engage in a meaningful literacy experience. Preschoolers benefit from hearing stories about people, places, and things that are meaningful to the children.

RESEARCH TO PRACTICE

Reading with Preschool English Learners

The practices listed here can be used with all preschool children, including English learners. Ongoing research promises to shed light on how each of these practices works with preschool English learners. The goal of these techniques is to encourage pleasurable interactions centered on books for both adults and children.

- Use "read-alouds" to encourage a group of young children to follow a story or text. For English learners small-group read-alouds ensure greater participation by each child in the group and allow the teacher to monitor learning for each child. Some bilingual teachers artfully use English and the home language in the reading and the discussion of the text or story (Thomas and Collier 2003b).

- Find ways to encourage children to use their home language to react to, predict, and review parts of a story or a passage when they are not yet at a level in their English-language development at which they can contribute in other ways. This approach increases English learners' experiences of inclusion and promotes other areas of cognitive and social development.

- Introduce key concepts or vocabulary in the children's home lan- guage and in English before reading a story or text to the children. Doing so will ensure that the children will gain familiarity, under- standing, and a connection with at least some of the story's or text's terminology or vocabulary.

- Review key or novel vocabulary through "text talk," in which the teacher identifies two or four words in the story or text. Each word is (1) read again as it was used in the text, and the children are asked to repeat the word along with the teacher to create a phonological representation of the word; (2) given a definition easily understood by preschoolers; and (3) used in a context other than that in the same story (Beck and McKeown 2001).

- Use dialogic reading with one child at a time or with a small group of children. In dialogic reading the adult (1) increases the number of times the child is asked to name objects in the pictures or drawings in picture books; (2) uses "what" and open-ended questions to encourage the child to say more than one word at a time; and (3) expands on the child's response as a way to teach vocabulary and provide more complete descriptions of what the child sees (Ameri- can Library Association 2004; Arnold and Whitehurst 1994).

Writing as a Part of Early Literacy

Offering opportunities to write, together with opportunities to read, is another important strategy for encouraging second-language learners to practice emerging skills in their new language while solidifying skills in their first language. The way children write depends on their language abilities and fine motor skills. Writing can take the form of drawing as a means to represent a thought, dictation to an adult, or beginning attempts at independent writing. English learners may use writing conventions taken from their home language and from English, much as they mix languages in their speech.

Here Alejandra, at five years of age and prior to entering kindergarten, uses both English and Spanish in a card she sent to her aunt, Tia Rebeca. (*Tia* is Spanish for aunt.)

Because of their common underlying metalinguistic awareness, bilingual individuals possess greater knowledge of language than do monolingual individuals. They have access to two languages and opportunities to contrast both. Apparently, this knowledge is related to an awareness of the meaning of written language. Among bilingual children awareness that spoken language can be represented in a written format has been found to develop earlier than it does among monolingual children (Bialystok 1997; Durgunoglu and Öney 2000). That is, awareness that sounds in the word *cookie* /k/ /oo/ /k/ /e/ are represented in letters "c" "o" "o" "k" "i" "e" is transferred from the first language and facilitates the acquisition of that awareness in the second language.

RESEARCH TO PRACTICE

Drawing on Students' Knowledge

The following quotation is an example of how one teacher used her students' prior knowledge of a topic to start a unit:

"This year the students and I explored the theme of 'The Ocean.' As an introductory activity I asked my students what type of fish they would like to be if they lived in the ocean. Since I have both Spanish speakers and English speakers, I asked and wrote the question in Spanish and English. The following are my questions and their answers:

What kind of fish would you like to be?

¿Que tipo de pez te gustaría ser?

John: *Tiburón* (shark)

Vivi: Red fish

Juan: *Una* tuna fish (a tuna fish)

Sara: *Un pescado rojo* (a red fish)

Toni: *Una ballena* (a whale)

Liliana: Goldfish, *la mamá* (goldfish, the mother)

Maria: *Un pez grande que nada en el mar todo el dia* (a big fish that swims in the sea all day long)

From their responses I could see that they already had a foundation of ocean animals, including some fairly advanced concepts, and vocabulary that I could build on."

Making Stories Come Alive

A key literacy practice for instructing English learners is to provide multiple ways for children to revisit the same text in other areas of the classroom or in other activities. This practice allows teachers and students to expand beyond read-alouds and to repeat and review story elements and vocabulary. Teachers can use flannel-board reenactments; puppet or doll-figure reenactments; story boxes with major props from the story; art and writing activities linked with the story; and home and family backpacks as well as songs and fingerplays related to the story to supplement the reading experience and make it come alive. Companion computer programs can serve to review the story, reinforce vocabulary, and provide an alternative means for children with disabilities to "read" alongside their peers. These purposeful, multi-sensory options for using different types of visual presentations and manipulatives can be used in small-group, individual, or whole-group instructional settings to provide different opportunities for English learners to interact with the story and contribute to further discussions (Isbell 2002).

Teachers adept at engaging English learners in purposeful, multisensory interactive lessons encourage students to think, question, listen, and reflect on elements of a story. Pinnegar, Teemant, and Tyra (2001) point out that it is important that children be placed in different types of combinations (e.g., a fluent English speaker with a bilingual speaker and with a home language speaker) because the very nature of the group will enhance or impede the risks the children are willing to take. For both monolingual and bilingual students, a comprehensive approach to early literacy should include instruction in the key subcomponents of the act of reading, including basic phonological awareness activities, such as rhyming and alliteration; exposure to alphabet and letter-sound correspondence; vocabulary development; and opportunities for beginning writing (Dickinson and Tabors 2001; International Reading Association 1998, 1999). Because a significant percentage of children, especially children at risk of having reading difficulties, benefit from systematic instruction, the key subcomponents of reading should be presented in small groups and should offer a sequence of purposeful, playful lessons (Astore 2004; Torgesen 2002).

Recently, an increasing number of scientifically validated studies conducted with school-age children have demonstrated the importance of preschool children being introduced to skills essential for learning to read early in elementary school (National Institute on Child Health and Human Development 2000). Learning activities that expose preschool children to the knowledge of letters, concepts of print, and basic phonological awareness work well when relatively brief, playful, engaging, multisensory, and purposeful (Neuman, Copple, and Bredekamp 2000). For preschool-age English learners, opportunities to begin learning those skills provide the foundation they need to learn to read and support their developing mastery of English. In creating opportunities for English learners to learn essential skills and have experiences leading to becoming skilled readers, teachers must attend to each child's developing ability to understand and speak English. English learners benefit from activities that foster essential skills and experiences in both English and their home language.

Recent studies indicate that teachers who produced the best results focused on developing decoding skills (e.g., alliteration, oral rhyming, and alphabetic knowledge), reading to the children, and engaging them in playful activities that develop oral language. Although many preschool teachers already implement several of these practices as part of their daily routine, some may wonder about how to fit these skill areas into a full schedule. The scientifically based research examined by the National Early Literacy Panel showed that addressing the majority of these skills for just a few minutes a day contributed to preschool children's progress with literacy (Strickland and others 2004). The panel also noted that early literacy is an area that merits further investigation, especially as it applies to English learners, who were the focus of only a handful of studies included in the panel's synthesis (Shanahan and Strickland 2004).

In another review of the research, Dickinson and Smith (2001) identified other contributing factors to children's literacy success, including (1) structural measures, such as teacher-child ratios, the size of the program, and the years of experience and educational levels of the teachers; (2) the educational process as assessed by rating tools, such as materials available to children, and the nature and organization of the furnishings; (3) teachers' beliefs about child development and appropriate classroom practices; and (4) teacher-child and child-child interactions. "The emotional tenor of classrooms is largely influenced by how teachers talk to individuals and the group. This emotional climate, in turn, has an impact on children's willingness to trust and to relate to teachers and to engage in literacy learning activities provided in the classroom" (Dickinson and Smith 2001, 140).

Literacy Strategies for English Learners with Special Needs

Introducing language and literacy experiences through concrete, multisensory approaches provides many children with disabilities with the support they need to build the foundation for decoding words

and understanding meaning. Having access to early literacy activities as part of the curriculum is the key to the educational success of all children, including children with mild to severe disabilities. Each child's unique learning needs should be considered in a comprehensive approach to early literacy.

Children with disabilities can benefit from exposure to short books with limited vocabulary. Researchers (Palincsar and Klenk 1992; Ruiz, Vargas, and Beltran 2002) have found that young English learners with mild to moderate disabilities can benefit from a literacy program that:

- Exposes children to letters, concepts of print, and basic phonological awareness skills

- Engages children and teachers in extended conversations

- Provides a flexible application of comprehension strategies

- Offers children opportunities to look through or be read a variety of books and stories

Although not focusing specifically on English learners, research has shown that children with Down syndrome benefit from sight-word recognition games along with attention to phonological awareness, vocabulary development, and comprehension (Al Otaiba and Hosp 2004). Similarly, young children with autism have benefited from being introduced to books with photographs (e.g., of cars, firefighters, children, and so forth), alphabet books, and books with informational text rather than make-believe stories (Richman 2003).

PRINCIPLES AND PRACTICES

10

PRINCIPLE

Offering a variety of opportunities for children to explore written materials and their meanings as well as the sounds of spoken language through rhyme and alliteration builds the language and literacy skills of preschool English learners.

The classroom should be rich with meaningful print to help children understand the connection between written and spoken language. Print is meaningful when it relates to children's immediate and past experiences. It is critical that literacy instruction include purposeful and playful activities.

PRACTICES

- Encourage the development of emergent literacy skills in a supportive environment by acknowledging and expanding on the children's efforts.

- Offer a rich variety of purposeful, playful, multisensory experiences with literacy and language, such as repetition accompanied by music or clapping (U.S. Department of Education 2002).

- Ask children and their parents to share with the class culturally relevant and teachable rhymes in their native languages to serve as tools for building the foundation for phonological awareness skills (Reading Rockets 2004).

- Relate literacy activities to the children's cultures, languages, and experiences to motivate the children's participation.

- Use pictures, photographs, and scenes in books as a platform for interaction and discussion.

- Help children recognize their names in print by encouraging them to watch as you print the letters of their names and say each letter as you write it. Display the children's names in various places in the classroom—by their cubbies, in artwork displayed on walls, in photo books with family pictures, for example (Armbruster and others 2003).

- Label items and learning centers in both English and the children's home languages, including sign language, picture symbols, and braille, when applicable to children in your class.

- Provide different types of reading materials throughout the classroom and outside instead of confining them to a single bookshelf. They may include menus, phone books, catalogs, magazines, posters, recipes, and written instructions for activities in addition to children's books.

- Provide different types of writing tools and materials, both indoors and outdoors, such as chalk, markers, pencils, crayons, feathers, sponges, stamps, paintbrushes, and droppers to promote writing throughout the daily routine. Remember to modify these materials with Velcro, vet wrap, or tubing for children with motor challenges.

- Remember to access the book collections in libraries, bookmobiles, families' homes, and other service agencies in the community. You may find a greater variety of books by borrowing from those sources.

- Communicate the importance of early reading and literacy activities to adults who interact with the children, including family members and classroom volunteers.

Attention to early literacy practices is essential to short-term and long-term outcomes for English learners. Because information on such practices is continually being generated, teachers are highly encouraged to continue to focus on best practices for young English learners as they pursue their professional development. In conclusion, the following "Research to Practice" chart provides examples of various early literacy practices children can engage in and explains how the practices found in many preschool classrooms relate to children's eventual success in reading and writing.

RESEARCH TO PRACTICE

Early Literacy Explorations

What Children Might Do	How Practice Relates to Reading and Writing
Make a pattern with objects such as buttons, beads, and small colored cubes.	By putting things in a certain order, children gain an understanding of sequence, helping them discover that the letters in words must go in a certain order.
Listen to a story, then talk with their families, teachers, or tutors and each other about the plot and characters, about what might happen next, and what they liked about the book.	Children enjoy read-aloud sessions, in which they learn that books can introduce people, places, and ideas and describe familiar experiences. Listening and talking help children build their vocabularies. They have fun while learning basic literacy concepts, such as that print is spoken words written down, that print carries meaning, and that text in many alphabetic languages is read from left to right, from the top to the bottom of a page, and from the front to the back of a book.
Play a matching game, such as concentration or picture bingo.	Seeing that some things are exactly the same leads children to understand that the letters in words must be written in the same order every time to convey meaning.

Source: Adapted from Koralek and Collins (1997, 13), with some elaboration of concepts based on Torgesen and Matheson (2001).

What Children Might Do	*How Practice Relates to Reading and Writing*
Move to music while following directions, such as, "Put your hands up, down, in front, in back, to the left, to the right. Now wiggle all over."	Children gain an understanding of such concepts as up/down, front/back, and left/right and add these words to their vocabularies. Understanding these concepts leads to knowledge of how words are read and written on a page and of positional terms.
Recite rhyming poems introduced by a parent, teacher, or tutor and make up new rhymes on their own.	Children develop one of the most important basic phonological awareness skills by learning about rhyming words.
Make signs for the "grocery store."	Children practice using print to provide information—in this case the price of different foods in meaningful contexts.
Retell a favorite story to another child or a stuffed animal.	Children gain confidence in their ability to learn to read. They practice telling the story in the order it was read to them—from the beginning to the middle to the end.
Use invented spelling to write a grocery list while a parent is writing his or her own list.	Children use writing to share information with others. By watching an adult write, they are introduced to the conventions of writing. Using invented spelling encourages the development of phonemic awareness.
Sign their names (with a scribble, a drawing, some of the letters, or "correctly") on an attendance chart, painting, or letter.	Children are learning that their names represent them and that other words represent objects, emotions, actions, and so on. They see that writing serves a purpose—for example, to let their teacher know they have arrived, to show others their artwork, or to tell someone who sent a letter.

Ask Yourself

1. How do my language and literacy goals for each child address both the child's home language and English?

2. How can I provide access to written materials throughout the classroom in English and the other languages used by my students?

3. Which strategies for becoming familiar with the literacy practices of the families of the children in my class have I implemented?

4. How extensively have I used the many resources available to me and to parents on this topic?

Additional References for Parents

Bishop, A., R. H. Yopp, and H. K. Yopp. 2000. *Ready for Reading: A Handbook for Parents of Preschoolers*. Boston, Mass.: Allyn and Bacon.

Hall, S. L., and L. C. Moats, 1999. *Straight Talk About Reading*. Chicago, Ill.: Contemporary Books.

Language Is the Key: A Program for Building Language and Literacy in Early Childhood. Seattle: Washington Learning Systems. Available in seven languages and in English with subtitles for viewers with hearing impairments. Available: http://www.walearning.com; or at (206) 310-7401.

Whitehurst, R. 2004. *Dialogic Reading: An Effective Way to Read to Preschoolers*. http://www.readingrockets.org/article.php?id=431

Additional References for Teachers

Center for the Improvement of Early Reading Achievement (CIERA) and the National Institute for Literacy (NIFL). 2001. *Put Reading First: The Research Building Blocks for Teaching Children to Read*. Washington, D.C.: Partnership for Reading. http://www.nifl.gov/partnershipforreading

"Learning to Read and Write: Developmentally Appropriate Practices for Young Children." 1998. A joint position statement of the International Reading Association and the National Association for the Education of Young Children. *The Reading Teacher*, Vol. 52, No. 2, 193–214.

Lindholm-Leary, K. 1999. *Biliteracy for a Global Society: An Idea Book on Dual Language Acquisition.* Washington, D.C.: National Clearing-house for Bilingual Education.

Report of the National Reading Panel. 2000. *Teaching Children to Read.* Rockville, Md.: NICHD Clearinghouse. Telephone 1-800-370-2943. http://www.nichd.nih.gov/publications/nrppubskey.cfm.

Note: See pages 115–28 for a list of works cited in this publication.

Appendix A
Principles for Promoting Language, Literacy, and Learning for Preschool English Learners

The ten principles that follow are included throughout this guide. Taken together, they foster an environment that respects and values linguistic and cultural diversity toward the eventual mastery of English.

1. The education of English learners is enhanced when preschool programs and families form meaningful partnerships.

2. Children benefit when their teachers understand cultural differences in language use and incorporate them into the daily routine.

3. Successful practices promote shared experiences in which language is used as a meaningful tool to communicate interests, ideas, and emotions.

4. Language development and learning are promoted when preschool teachers and children creatively and interactively use language.

5. Experimenting with the use, form, purpose, and intent of the first and second languages leads to growth in acquiring the second language.

6. Continued use and development of the child's home language will benefit the child as he or she acquires English.

7. Code switching is a normal part of language development for many bilingual children.

8. Coordination and collaboration among families, teachers, and specialists become crucial in supporting the language and literacy development of children with disabilities and other special needs.

9. Engaging in multiple literacy practices, such as reading books, singing songs, and reciting poetry, is part of the daily life of many families.

10. Offering a variety of opportunities for children to explore written materials and their meanings as well as the sounds of spoken language through rhyme and alliteration builds the language and literacy skills of preschool English learners.

Appendix B
Prekindergarten Learning and Development Guidelines

The reader is encouraged to refer to the source from which the following guidelines are taken: *Prekindergarten Learning and Development Guidelines* (California Department of Education 2000). Because all the areas of children's learning and development are interrelated, all of the items listed are integral to the optimal growth and development of young English learners.

Program Foundations

Planning the Preschool Environment

1. The environment is safe and comfortable for children and adults.

2. The environment is arranged to maximize learning, facilitate movement, minimize distractions, and organize children's play.

3. The materials in the environment are interesting, engaging, and age appropriate.

4. The environment is supportive of diverse cultures.

5. The environment welcomes parents and provides a place for communication between staff and parents.

6. The environment is accessible to children with disabilities and other special needs.

7. The environment makes appropriate use of technology.

Addressing Cultural Diversity

1. The program encourages and supports appreciation of and respect for individual and group similarities and differences, making the acceptance of diversity a theme that is central to the classroom culture.

2. Program materials reflect the characteristics, values, and practices of diverse cultural groups.

3. Whenever reasonable, teachers engage in practices consistent with those from the children's homes.

4. Teachers attempt, as much as possible, to learn about the history, beliefs, and practices of the children and the families they serve, and they receive support for their efforts from the early care and education center.

5. Children are encouraged to recognize and develop strategies to use when they encounter social injustice, bias, and prejudice.

Planning for Assessment

1. Assessment is done to benefit the children and to enhance the effectiveness of parents and teachers.

2. Assessment includes multiple sources of information and is balanced across cognitive, social, emotional, and health domains.

3. Assessment takes place in a context or setting that is natural, nonthreatening, and familiar to the children.

4. Assessment is continuous and is used regularly for planning and developing specific strategies to support the children's learning and development.

5. Assessment for admission or placement purposes has few appropriate uses in preschool; but, if done, it should have an established reliability and validity, and it should be conducted by trained examiners.

6. Programs direct significant efforts toward developing assessments that are accurate, fair, and free of cultural bias.

7. As much as possible, parents are aware of and are involved in assessments of their children.

Including Children with Disabilities or Other Special Needs

1. Teachers accept and actively support the concept of inclusion by creating a classroom environment in which all the children and their families feel that they are welcome.

2. Teachers are part of the educational team that develops and implements individualized education programs (IEPs) for children eligible to receive special education services.

3. Teachers work collaboratively with other specialists to determine appropriate modifications in the curriculum, instructional methods, or classroom environment.

4. Programs provide sufficient release time, training information, and support for teachers to plan and consult regarding children with disabilities or other special needs.

5. Teachers work closely with families in an educational partnership and provide them with appropriate information and support.

Involving Parents and Families

1. The teacher incorporates parents' goals into program instruction and supports the involvement of parents in helping their children to attain those goals.

2. The program creates an environment where parents feel empowered and comfortable in speaking up for their children.

3. The program regularly provides parents with information about activities in the program and about their children's learning and development.

4. The teacher recognizes the role that various family members other than parents may play in promoting children's development.

5. The program supports and is an advocate for strong families.

Organizing Staff Preparation and Development Programs

1. The program has a comprehensive staff development plan.

2. The program provides adequate paid time for professional development activities.

3. The program promotes professionalism and ethical behavior.

4. The program provides opportunities for all staff to participate in decision making.

5. The program provides tools and materials needed by the staff members to advance their professional skills and knowledge.

6. The program employs staff who meet the requirements for education and experience for their positions and encourages advancement along a planned career pathway.

7. The program has a compensation schedule that acknowledges and validates the required training and experience of each staff member.

8. Professional development activities stress the development of cultural competence.

9. The program supports professional development activities that focus on family involvement.

10. The staff development plan incorporates a clearly defined approach to integrating technology into the early childhood program.

Curriculum

Social and Emotional Development

1. The staff is responsive to the children's emotional needs.

2. The program climate, organization, and routine create a sense of safety, security, and predictability.

3. Each child is helped to develop a sense of self-worth and capability.

4. Each child is helped to develop a sense of self as a valued and responsible member of the group.

5. The children are guided and helped to form and maintain satisfying relationships with others.

6. The children are guided and helped to express their emotions in socially acceptable ways.

7. The children's social and cultural backgrounds are taken into account in interpreting the children's preferences and behaviors in the preschool setting.

8. The children's social behavior is guided in the context of daily activities.

9. The goal of discipline is to promote greater social and emotional competence.

Language and Literacy Development

1. Programs support development in both language and literacy.

2. Programs provide a language-rich and print-rich environment to support the children's language and literacy learning across curricular areas.

3. Adults model language and literacy practices to enhance the children's learning and development in those areas.

4. Programs implement a language arts curriculum that lays the foundation for the children's success in language arts in elementary school.

5. The program recognizes and includes the home languages of English learners.

6. The children's language and literacy development is supported through interaction between preschool staff and the children's families.

Mathematical Learning and Development

1. The program develops and builds on the children's existing informal mathematical knowledge, recognizing that children enter preschool with different experiences in mathematics.

2. Teacher-guided and child-initiated activities are integrated into a mathematically rich learning environment using multiple instructional approaches.

3. The program implements a mathematics curriculum that lays the foundation for the children's success in mathematics in elementary school.

4. The program identifies clear, age-appropriate goals for mathematics learning and development.

5. The program establishes a partnership with parents and other caregivers in preparing the children for mathematics learning.

Physical and Motor Development

1. The curriculum gives attention to all areas of motor skill development, including gross motor, fine motor, oral motor, and sensorimotor.

2. Consideration is given to the children's varying rates of development and acquisition of skills.

3. The program provides many opportunities for free play.

4. Teachers consider the children's special health and physical needs when designing physical activities.

Other Curriculum Areas

The teacher builds on the natural curiosity that children have about the world around them by creating opportunities for the exploration of history–social science, science, the arts, and health and nutrition. These subjects are part of the program's daily routines and are fully integrated into the program. Where appropriate, the program links those content areas with other content areas, such as social-emotional development, language and literacy development, mathematics, and physical and motor development.

Appendix C
Desired Results for Children and Families

The California Department of Education's Child Development Division has revised its approach to evaluating the child care and development services it provides. It is moving away from a process-oriented compliance model and toward a focus on the results desired from the system. This approach, which is compatible with the Department's accountability system for elementary and secondary education, is intended to improve the results achieved for children and families through the child development services provided. Titled Desired Results for Children and Families, the new system will document the progress made by children and families in achieving the desired results and will provide information to help practitioners improve their child care and development services. Specific guidance on how best to use the Desired Results system with English learners is being developed by Berkeley Evaluation and Assessment Research, University of California, Berkeley. The new system is designed to:

- Identify measures demonstrating the achievement of desired results across the development areas for children from birth to age thirteen in child care and development programs.

- Provide information that reflects the contributions made by each of the various types of Department-funded child development programs in achieving the desired results.

- Hold programs accountable to program standards that support the achievement of desired results and are used to measure program quality.

- Provide a data-collection mechanism for evaluating the quality of individual child development programs.

- Create a base of information on the relationships between processes and results that can be used to target technical assistance for improving practices in all child development programs.

The intent of the Desired Results system at the state level is to identify successes and areas for improvement so that the Child Development Division can provide support and technical assistance to increase program quality. At the program level the extent to which children and families are achieving the desired results will be determined so that quality improvement activities are effectively targeted to benefit

Source: Desired Results Web site: http://www.sonoma.edu/cihs/desiredresults/training

program participants directly. Differences in the structure and objectives of individual programs will be acknowledged, and the system will be culturally sensitive and linguistically responsive to the diverse populations of children and families served.

The primary objective of the Desired Results approach is to encourage progress toward the achievement of those results by providing information and technical assistance to improve program quality. The system has been built on existing processes and procedures, with an emphasis on the coordination of programs and services to support the continuum of children's developmental progress from birth to age thirteen.

The Desired Results system also interfaces with a concurrent project, the Desired Results: Access for Children with Disabilities Project (DR Access). That project is funded through the Early Education Unit, Special Education Division, California Department of Education, and is being conducted by the California Institute on Human Services, Sonoma State University. The DR Access Project coordinates with Desired Results in two ways. First, DR Access staff worked with the Child Development Division and their contractors during the development of the Desired Results framework to make the Desired Results Developmental Profile as inclusive and appropriate as possible for the assessment of the progress of young children with disabilities. DR Access staff have also developed a system of adaptations and guidelines for the Desired Results Developmental Profile that will allow practitioners to assess children with disabilities in an appropriate manner within the structure of the Desired Results system.

Through these two approaches the DR Access Project ensures that the Desired Results framework considers the needs of young children with disabilities and is applicable to all settings where children with disabilities and their families are served, including both regular and special education placements. The vision held by the contributors to the Desired Results system and the DR Access Project is that through this collaborative effort a continuity of outcomes will be achieved for all children in California Department of Education programs.

The training and implementation phase of the Desired Results system for center-based programs and family child care home networks is being carried out with a series of regional training sessions for local program administrators. Assisted by California Institute on Human Services, the Child Development Division is providing comprehensive training designed to facilitate implementation of the Desired Results system in programs at the local level and to build the capacity of local programs to train staff who work directly with children. Participation in the training is by invitation only. The sites are selected one year prior to a scheduled coordinated compliance review or contract monitoring review.

Components of the Desired Results Structure

There are four basic components of the Desired Results structure: the results themselves, indicators, measures, and measurement tools. The six desired results to which all California Department of Education-funded child care and development programs are expected to contribute are listed as follows:

- The children are personally and socially competent.
- The children are effective learners.
- The children show physical and motor competence.
- The children are safe and healthy.
- Families support their children's learning and development.
- Families achieve their goals.

The desired results for children encompass the four developmental domains (i.e., cognitive, social-emotional, language, and physical development), which are reflected and integrated throughout the indicators, measures, and examples of the measures.

A *desired result* is defined as a condition of well-being for children or families (e.g., that children are personally and socially competent), expressing the positive impact of the entire system on the development and functioning of children and on the self-sufficiency and functioning of families.

An *indicator* defines a desired result more specifically so that it can be measured. For example, as an indicator of the desired result that children are personally and socially competent, children show self-awareness and a positive self-concept. Desired results are generally better measured by using multiple indicators, none of which gives full information on all aspects of achievement.

A *measure* quantifies achievement of a particular indicator (e.g., that a preschooler can communicate easily with familiar adults).

A *measurement tool* is the actual instrument or procedure used to capture or track information on indicators and standards of achievement (e.g., the Desired Results Developmental Profile).

Appendix D
Transition to Kindergarten or Elementary School

Preschool English learners eventually reach the age at which they transition into the kindergarten through grade twelve school system. Preschool teachers need to know how best to prepare these young children to be cognitively, socially, and emotionally ready for this next educational environment. This appendix provides a brief discussion of the transition process and helpful transition strategies as well as an overview of California's English-language development standards and English–language arts development standards for kindergarten. Knowing what comes next is essential for teachers, parents, and administrators as they work to help young preschool English learners make a successful transition to school.

What Makes the Transition to School Go Smoothly for Young Children and Their Families?

Several practices help ensure a smooth placement and adjustment for children moving from preschool to kindergarten or first grade. They include strategies and procedures that (1) provide continuity through activities that build bridges between home, early childhood education, and school experiences; and (2) connect the child development, health and social services, family partnerships and involvement services, and education systems for children from birth to age five. Effective transition activities address children's social, emotional, physical, cultural, linguistic, and cognitive development; involve families; prepare children for the transition to school; and link preschool and elementary school educators (Hand 2004).

Specific strategies that contribute to children's successful transitions to school include having:

- Preschool children meet their kindergarten teacher before the start of the school year.
- Preschool children practice school routines and behavioral expectations.
- Preschool children be introduced to future peers.
- Preschool children visit their kindergarten classroom or setting.
- New kindergartners feel welcomed by being enabled to experience elements of practice from their preschool setting.
- Children and families experience continuity of early intervention services between the preschool and elementary school.

The K–3 English-Language Development and English–Language Arts Standards

The foundation for developing English reading skills for all students is a solid initial understanding of the relationships between English sounds and letters—the relationships between the spoken and the written language. For the English learner this understanding is first developed through the recognition and production of English sounds. Students begin this process most effectively by first learning the English sounds that exist in their first language and then those that do not. They are then taught to transfer that knowledge to the printed language. As students develop knowledge of the correspondence between sounds and printed symbols, they develop skills to analyze English morphemes (i.e., prefixes, suffixes, root words, and so on). These skills in word analysis are some of the building blocks students need to develop fluency in English and literacy skills.

The California *Reading/Language Arts Framework* specifies that teachers must provide students with straightforward assessments of their proficiency in English at every stage of instruction so that the students understand what they must do to improve. As stated throughout this resource guide, the processes by which students develop proficiency in a second language differ from the experiences of monolingual English speakers. For example, grammatical structures that monolingual English speakers learn early in their language development may be learned much later by students learning English as a second language. The *English-Language Development Standards* (ELD) provides teachers with usable information to ensure that English-language development is occurring appropriately for all students (California Department of Education 2002).

For kindergarten through grade two, the English–language arts (ELA) standards on phonemic awareness, concepts about print, and decoding and word recognition have been integrated into the *English–Language Arts Content Standards* (California Department of Education 1998). The standards for kindergarten, which serve as anchor points that can be used to determine whether English learners are making appropriate progress toward becoming proficient readers of English, are presented as follows:

Kindergarten English–Language Arts Content Standards

READING

1.0 Word Analysis, Fluency, and Systematic Vocabulary Development

Students know about letters, words, and sounds. They apply this knowledge to read simple sentences.

Concepts About Print

1.1 Identify the front cover, back cover, and title page of a book.
1.2 Follow words from left to right and from top to bottom on the printed page.
1.3 Understand that printed materials provide information.
1.4 Recognize that sentences in print are made up of separate words.
1.5 Distinguish letters from words.
1.6 Recognize and name all uppercase and lowercase letters of the alphabet.

Phonemic Awareness

1.7 Track (move sequentially from sound to sound) and represent the number, sameness/difference, and order of two and three isolated phonemes (e.g., /f, s, th/, /j, d, j/).
1.8 Track (move sequentially from sound to sound) and represent changes in simple syllables and words with two and three sounds as one sound is added, substituted, omitted, shifted, or repeated (e.g., vowel-consonant, consonant-vowel, or consonant-vowel-consonant).
1.9 Blend vowel-consonant sounds orally to make words or syllables.
1.10 Identify and produce rhyming words in response to an oral prompt.
1.11 Distinguish orally stated one-syllable words and separate into beginning or ending sounds.
1.12 Track auditorily each word in a sentence and each syllable in a word.
1.13 Count the number of sounds in syllables and syllables in words.

Decoding and Word Recognition

1.14 Match all consonant and short-vowel sounds to appropriate letters.
1.15 Read simple one-syllable and high-frequency words (i.e., sight words).
1.16 Understand that as letters of words change, so do the sounds (i.e., the alphabetic principle).

Vocabulary and Concept Development

   1.17   Identify and sort common words in basic categories (e.g., colors, shapes, foods).

   1.18   Describe common objects and events in both general and specific language.

2.0   Reading Comprehension

Students identify the basic facts and ideas in what they have read, heard, or viewed. They use comprehension strategies (e.g., generating and responding to questions, comparing new information to what is already known). The selections in *Recommended Literature: Kindergarten Through Grade Twelve* (California Department of Education 2002) illustrate the quality and complexity of the materials to be read by students.

Structural Features of Informational Materials

   2.1   Locate the title, table of contents, name of author, and name of illustrator.

Comprehension and Analysis of Grade-Level-Appropriate Text

   2.2   Use pictures and context to make predictions about story content.

   2.3   Connect to life experiences the information and events in texts.

   2.4   Retell familiar stories.

   2.5   Ask and answer questions about essential elements of a text.

3.0   Literary Response and Analysis

Students listen and respond to stories based on well-known characters, themes, plots, and settings. The selections in *Recommended Literature: Kindergarten Through Grade Twelve* illustrate the quality and complexity of the materials to be read by students.

Narrative Analysis of Grade-Level-Appropriate Text

   3.1   Distinguish fantasy from realistic text.

   3.2   Identify types of everyday print materials (e.g., storybooks, poems, newspapers, signs, labels).

   3.3   Identify characters, settings, and important events.

WRITING

1.0   Writing Strategies

Students write words and brief sentences that are legible.

Organization and Focus

   1.1   Use letters and phonetically spelled words to write about experiences, stories, people, objects, or events.

1.2 Write consonant-vowel-consonant words (i.e., demonstrate the alphabetic principle).

1.3 Write by moving from left to right and from top to bottom.

Penmanship

1.4 Write uppercase and lowercase letters of the alphabet independently, attending to the form and proper spacing of the letters.

WRITTEN AND ORAL ENGLISH LANGUAGE CONVENTIONS

The standards for written and oral English language conventions have been placed between those for writing and for listening and speaking because those conventions are essential to both sets of skills.

1.0 Written and Oral English Language Conventions

Students write and speak with a command of standard English conventions.

Sentence Structure

1.1 Recognize and use complete, coherent sentences when speaking.

Spelling

1.2 Spell independently by using prephonetic knowledge, sounds of the alphabet, and knowledge of letter names.

LISTENING AND SPEAKING

1.0. Listening and Speaking Strategies

Students listen and respond to oral communication. They speak in clear and coherent sentences.

Comprehension

1.1 Understand and follow one- and two-step oral directions.

1.2 Share information and ideas, speaking audibly in complete, coherent sentences.

2.0. Speaking Applications (Genres and Their Characteristics)

Students deliver brief recitations and oral presentations about familiar experiences or interests, demonstrating command of the organization and delivery strategies outlined in Listening and Speaking Standard 1.0.

Using the listening and speaking strategies of kindergarten outlined in Listening and Speaking Standard 1.0, students:

2.1 Describe people, places, things (e.g., size, color, shape), locations, and actions.

2.2 Recite short poems, rhymes, and songs.

2.3 Relate an experience or creative story in a logical sequence.

The lists of ELD and ELA standards are lengthy since they contain overarching goals and more specific learning objectives similar to the kindergarten ELA standards listed previously. Teachers and programs are encouraged to obtain the entire ELD and ELA standards documents.

WestEd's Northern California Comprehensive Assistance Center has developed a publication titled *The Map of Standards for English Learners* that presents the two sets of standards, ELD and ELA, in an easy-to-follow tabular format. Excerpts from the document are presented on the following pages:

ELD Standards / ELA Standards

Cluster	Level	ELD Standards — K–2	ELA Standards — K	ELA Standards — 1	ELA Standards — 2
6		**Retell Stories and Summarize Main Idea**	2.3 Relate an experience or creative story in a logical sequence.	2.2 Retell stories, using basic story grammar and relating the sequence of story events by answering who, what, when, where, and how questions.	1.7 Recount experiences in a logical sequence.
	EI	Retell familiar stories and short conversations by using appropriate gestures, expressions, and illustrative objects.			2.1 Recount experiences or present stories.
	I	Retell stories and talk about school-related activities by using expanded vocabulary, descriptive words, and paraphrasing.		2.3 Relate an important life event or personal experience in a simple sequence.	1.8 Retell stories, including characters, setting, and plot.
	EA	Retell stories in greater detail by including the characters, setting, and plot. **(ES*)**			
	A	Narrate and paraphrase events in greater detail by using more extended vocabulary. (2)		2.4 Provide descriptions, with careful attention to sensory detail.	
7		**Recite Rhymes and Stories**	2.2 Recite short poems, rhymes, and songs.	2.1 Recite poems, rhymes, songs, and stories.	
	EI	Recite familiar rhymes, songs, and simple stories.			
8		**Ask and Answer Questions**	2.1 Describe people, places, things (e.g., size, color, shape), locations, and actions.	1.2 Ask questions for clarification and understanding.	1.2 Ask for clarification and explanation of stories and ideas.
	B	Answer simple questions with one- to two-word responses.			
	EI	Ask and answer questions by using phrases or simple sentences. **(ES*)**			

Levels: B = Beginning; EI = Early Intermediate; I = Intermediate; EA = Early Advanced; A = Advanced
Essential Standards: ES = Essential ELA and matching ELD standards (major emphasis in CST and CAHSEE); ES* = Essential ELD standards on CELDT

From J. Carr and R. Lagunoff, *The Map of Standards for English Learners: Integrating Instruction and Assessment of English–Language Development and English–Language Arts Standards in California* (Fourth edition), copyright © 2003 WestEd. Reprinted by permission of WestEd, San Francisco. http://www.wested.org/cs/wew/view/rs/719

ELD Standards

ELA Standards

Cluster	Level	ELD Standards (K–2)	ELA K	ELA 1	ELA 2
	I	Ask and answer instructional questions by using simple sentences.			1.5 Organize presentations to maintain a clear focus.
	EA	Ask and answer instructional questions with more extensive supporting elements (e.g., "Which part of the story was the most important?").			1.9 Report on a topic with supportive facts and details.
					2.2 Report on a topic with facts and details, drawing from several sources of information.
1 ES		**Use Vocabulary for Communication**			
	B	Retell simple stories by using drawings, words, or phrases.	(See Listening and Speaking, Speaking Applications.)	(See Listening and Speaking, Speaking Applications.)	(See Listening and Speaking, Speaking Applications.)
	B	Respond appropriately to some social and academic interactions (e.g., simple question/answer, negotiate play).			
	B	Demonstrate comprehension of simple vocabulary with an appropriate action. **(ES*)**			
	B	Produce simple vocabulary (single words or short phrases) to communicate basic needs in social and academic situations (e.g., locations, greetings, classroom objects).			
	EI	Produce vocabulary, phrases, and simple sentences to communicate basic needs in social and academic situations.			

ELD Standards

Cluster	Level	K–2	K	1	2
	I	Use more complex vocabulary and sentences to communicate needs and express ideas in a wider variety of social and academic settings (e.g., classroom discussions, mediation of conflicts).			
	I	Apply knowledge of content-related vocabulary to discussions and reading. (ES*)			
	I	Describe common objects and events in both general and specific language. (ES)	1.8 Same as ELD standard. (ES)		1.8 Same as ELD standard. (ES)
2ES	B	**Use Social and Academic Vocabulary** Read aloud simple words (e.g., nouns and adjectives) in stories or games.	2.2 Recite short poems, rhymes, and songs.	2.1 Recite poems, rhymes, songs, and stories.	
	EI	Read simple vocabulary, phrases, and sentences independently. (ES*)			
	EI	Read aloud an increasing number of English words.			
	I	Use decoding skills to read more complex words independently.			
	EA	Use decoding skills and knowledge of academic and social vocabulary to begin independent reading.			
	A	Apply knowledge of academic and social vocabulary to achieve independent reading. (2)			
	A	Use knowledge of individual words in unknown compound words to predict their meaning. (2) (ES)			

ELA Standards

Additional References

California Department of Education. 1999. *Reading/Language Arts Framework for California Public Schools, Kindergarten Through Grade Twelve* (with content standards). Sacramento: California Department of Education.

Carr, J., and R. Lagunoff. 2003. *The Map of Standards for English Learners: Integrating Instruction and Assessment of English-Language Development and English–Language Arts Standards in California* (Fourth edition). San Francisco: WestEd. http://wested.org/cs/wew/view/rs/719

Hand, A. 2004. *Transition to School: An Important Focus for School Readiness Programs.* First 5 California Implementation Tools for School Readiness Series. Los Angeles: UCLA Center for Healthier Children, Families, and Communities. This resource also includes strategies for family support and community linkages during transition. http://www.healthychild.ucla.edu or http://www.ccfc.ca.gov

Note: See pages 115–28 for a list of works cited in this publication.

Glossary

academic English: The variety of English used in schools, in textbooks, and in many business and government transactions.

American Sign Language: A complex visual-spatial language used by the deaf community in the United States and in English-speaking parts of Canada. There are also other systems of signed communication, such as Signed English. Children from other countries may have learned their own regional variation of a signed language.

augmentative communication: Any method of communicating without speech, such as the use of signs, gestures, and electronic and nonelectronic devices.

bilingual: Refers to a person (child or adult) who speaks two languages.

biliterate: Having the knowledge and skill needed to read and write in one's home language and in a second language.

cerebral palsy: A disorder of posture, muscle tone, and movement resulting from brain damage.

code switching: The practice of using more than one language to express a thought or idea.

cognate: One of two or more words having the same linguistic root or origin.

content knowledge: The concepts, principles, relationships, processes, and applications of an academic subject that children should know. The developmental age and grade level of the children should determine the extent of the knowledge expected.

cross-language transfer: The skills, background knowledge, and cognitive strategies that children transfer between their first and second languages.

culture: Values, ideas, and other symbolic, meaningful systems created and transmitted by a group of people.

decoding: The ability to translate symbols (e.g., alphabet letters) into recognizable syllables and words. It is grounded in an understanding of the mechanics of text (*concepts about print*), the knowledge that spoken words consist of a sequence of individual sounds or phonemes (*phonemic awareness*), a familiarity with the letters in the language (*letter knowledge*), the knowledge that the letters in the written words represent corresponding sounds (*alphabetic principle*), and the ability to bring these elements together to decipher regular words.

Down syndrome: A common genetic disorder in which a child is born with 47 rather than 46 chromosomes, resulting in developmental delays, mental retardation, low muscle tone, and other possible effects.

dual-language development: The development of two languages; same as bilingual-language development.

early literacy: The knowledge and skills that are the forerunners to later success in reading and writing.

emergent readers: Children who have some early literacy skills but are not yet fluent readers.

English learners: Children attending school in the United States who come from a home where a language other than English is spoken.

expressive language: The process of formulating and sending a message. One way to express language is through speech. Other ways are through using sign language, pointing to words and pictures on a communication board, and using written messages on a computer screen.

formulaic speech: Speech characterized by formulas or chunks and phrases that the child uses without completely understanding how they function in the language.

grammar: The system of rules by which words are formed and put together to make sentences.

home language: The language used primarily by the child's family in the home environment. For some children there may be more than one home language (e.g., when the mother speaks Chinese and the father speaks English).

hypothesis: A tentative explanation for a phenomenon used as a basis for further investigation.

hypothesize: To offer something as a form of hypothesis.

immigrant experience: An individual's or a family's experience of leaving one's home country and moving to a new country.

indigenous: Having origins in a region or a country.

individualized education program: A written plan constituting a legal document that states a child's present level of functioning; specific areas that need special services; annual goals; short-term objectives; services to be provided; and the method of evaluation to be implemented for children three to twenty-one years of age who have been determined eligible for special education (Cook, Klein, and Tessier 2004).

individualized family service plan: Both a process and a document. The process consists of the gathering, sharing, and exchanging of information between families and staff to enable families to make informed choices about the early intervention services they want for their children. The document is a written contract outlining outcome statements to be achieved by the infant or toddler with special needs and his or her family (Cook, Klein, and Tessier 2004).

language: The human use of spoken or written words as a communication system. Language can also include a system of communication based on signs, gestures, or inarticulate sounds.

language acquisition: The process of learning a language. Assuming the absence of a disability and the presence of spoken language, children subconsciously acquire the basics of their home language (phonology, morphology, syntax, semantics, pragmatics) from birth through age five. From age six and continuing throughout adulthood, they continue this subconscious learning, adding layers of complexity to what they already know. Each grade level of formal school instruction adds to the cognitive complexity of developing spoken and written language.

language brokers: Children who use their developing bilingual language skills to act as translators between institutions and their family members and to assist their peers or siblings who may not know as much English as they do.

language loss: Depletion of language occurring when a member of the minority group can no longer use the minority language as well as he or she used to do or when some of the proficiency is no longer accessible. Language loss may also refer to incomplete or imperfect learning of a language spoken in childhood.

metalinguistic awareness: An awareness of the structure and function of language that allows one to reflect and consciously manipulate the language.

monolingual: Refers to a person (child or adult) who speaks one language.

morphology: The study of meaningful units of language and their combination to form words.

motherese: The name given to the restricted sort of language spoken by mothers and other primary caregivers to their young children, the main function of which is to teach the children the basic function and structure of language. Adults make an unconscious effort to stretch the signals, exaggerating the acoustic components that are exactly the dimensions that the baby needs to pay attention to in order to form the mental maps for speech.

multilingual: Refers to a person (child or adult) who speaks more than one language.

overgeneralization: A language practice used by children as they are learning a language in which they apply a perceived rule or use of a word incorrectly. For example, a child may say "mans" instead of "men" to show the plural form of the word "man."

phonemic awareness: The ability to hear, identify, and manipulate the sequence of individual sounds (phonemes) in spoken words.

phonics: Instructional practices that emphasize how spellings are related to speech sounds in systematic ways; letter-sound correspondences.

phonological awareness: A sensitivity to the sounds in spoken language. Basic levels of phonological awareness activities include listening to, recognizing, and completing rhymes; segmenting spoken words in sentences and syllables in words; and recognizing onset and rhyme in word families (e.g., rat, pat, chat).

phonology: The system or pattern of speech sounds used in a particular language.

pragmatic/communicative competence: The ability to understand and apply social rules for language use. Children who are skilled at pragmatic use or have communicative competence can use language to persuade peers and adults, ask and answer questions in school, and request entry into a playgroup.

private speech: The practice of children talking aloud to themselves while engaged in play.

receptive language: The process of receiving and understanding a message through language.

register: Different forms of the same language that are used with certain people or in certain situations.

scaffolding: A process by which adults or capable peers provide supportive structures to help children learn and play. Scaffolding occurs at a time when children are faced with a challenge that they can solve with a simple hint, question, or prompt.

script: The way a language is represented in writing. For example, Armenian script looks like this: Հայկական. Chinese script looks like this: 黃帝. Arabic script looks like this: شٌ. English script is represented in the writing in this guide.

second-language acquisition: The process by which a child or an adult learns to understand and use a second language.

semantics: The study of how meaning in language is created by the use and interrelationships of words, phrases, and sentences.

simultaneous language acquisition, simultaneous bilingualism: The process of learning two languages at the same time.

social English: The variety of English initially used by most speakers learning English as a second language in informal situations and conversations.

sociocultural perspective: Based on the work of Vygotsky, sociocultural theory presents the perspective that children's cognitive structures are developed through the actions and speech of their caretakers and are transmitted through social interactions. It follows then that there will be culturally coded styles of speech and interaction which will result in culturally related patterns of thought.

successive language acquisition, successive bilingualism: The process of learning a second language after the first language has already been learned or after basic mastery in the first language has been achieved.

syntax: The ordering of and relationship between the words and other structural elements in phrases and sentences.

take the floor: The act of calling attention to oneself to participate or show one's knowledge; being the main speaker in a group.

telegraphic speech: Speech characterized by the use of a few content words without functional words or certain grammatical markers, as in telegraphs.

theory: The body of rules, ideas, principles, and techniques that applies to a particular subject.

vocabulary: All the words used by or known by a child or adult. *Oral vocabulary* refers to words used in speaking or recognized in listening. *Reading vocabulary* refers to words recognized or used in print.

wait time: The amount of time a teacher allows for children to respond to a question or request.

Works Cited

Ada, A. F., and I. Campoy. 2003. *Pío peep! Traditional Spanish Nursery Rhymes.* New York: Harper Collins.

Al Otaiba, S., and M. K. Hosp. 2004. "Providing Effective Literacy Instruction to Students with Down Syndrome," *Teaching Exceptional Children,* Vol. 36, No. 4, 28–35.

American Library Association. 2004. *The Dialogic Reading Program for Parents of 2- and 3-Year-Olds.* http://www.ala.org/ala/pla/plaissues/earlylit/workshopspartent/dialogicreading.htm

Armbruster, B., and others. 2003. *A Child Becomes a Reader, Birth Through Preschool: Proven Ideas for Research for Parents.* Available in English and Spanish at the Partnership for Reading Web site: http://www.nifl.gov/partnershipforreading; or by e-mail at edpubs@net.ed.gov; or at 1-800-228-8813.

Arnold, D. S., and G. J. Whitehurst. 1994. "Accelerating Language Development Through Picture Book Reading: A Summary of Dialogic Reading and its Effect," in *Bridges to Literacy: Approaches to Supporting Child and Family Literacy.* Edited by D. Dickinson. Cambridge, Mass.: Basil Blackwell.

Artiles, A. J., and A.A. Ortiz, editors. *English Language Learners with Special Education Needs: Identification, Assessment, and Instruction.* McHenry, Ill.: Center for Applied Linguistics and Delta Systems.

Ashworth, M., and H. P. Wakefield. 2004. *Teaching the World's Children: ESL for Ages Three to Seven.* Toronto: Pippin.

Astore, M. 2004. "Building Language and Literacy: Essential Experiences for Preschoolers," *Building Bridges,* Vol. 9, No. 1, 2–7.

August, D.; M. Calderón; and M. Carlo. 2002. *Transfer of Skills from Spanish to English: A Study of Young Learners.* Washington, D.C.: Center for Applied Linguistics.

August, D., and K. Hakuta, editors. 1997. *Improving Schooling for Language-Minority Children: A Research Agenda.* Washington, D.C.: National Academy Press.

Baddeley, A. 1988. "Cognitive Psychology and Human Memory," *Trends in Neurosciences,* Vol. 11, 176–81.

Baker, C. 2000a. *A Parent's and Teacher's Guide to Bilingualism* (Second edition). Clevedon, England: Multilingual Matters.

Baker, C. 2000b. *The Care and Education of Young Bilinguals: An Introduction to Professionals.* Clevedon, England: Multilingual Matters.

Baquedano-Lopez, P. 2003. "Language, Literacy, and Community," in *Handbook of Early Childhood Literacy.* Edited by N. Hall, J. Larson, and J. Marsh. Thousand Oaks, Calif.: Sage Publications.

Barrera, R., and R. Jiménez. 2002. *The Role of Literacy in Culturally and Linguistically Diverse Student Learning.* Washington, D.C.: National Clearinghouse on Bilingual Education, George Washington University.

Barrera, R. B.; R. Quiroa; and R. Valdivia. 2002. "Spanish in Latino Picture Storybooks in English: Its Use and Textual Effects," in *Multicultural Issues in Literacy Research and Practice.* Edited by A. Willis and others. Mahwah, N.J.: Lawrence Erlbaum.

Beck, I. L., and M. G. McKeown. 2001. "Text Talk: Capturing Benefits for Read-aloud Experiences for Young Children," *The Reading Teacher,* Vol. 55, 10–20.

Ben-Zeev, L. O. 1997. "The Influence of Bilingualism on Cognitive Strategy and Cognitive Development," *Child Development,* Vol. 48, 1009–18.

Berg, M., and T. Stegelman. 2003. "The Critical Role of Phonological and Phonemic Awareness in Reading Success: A Model for Early Literacy in Rural Schools," *Rural Special Education Quarterly,* Vol. 22, No. 4, 47–54.

Bergert, S., and J. Burnette. 2000. *Educating Exceptional Children: A Statistical Profile.* Arlington, Va.: ERIC Clearinghouse on Disabilities and Gifted Education. ERIC Documentation Reproduction Service No. ED-99-CO-0026.

Berk, L. E. 2003. *Child Development* (Sixth edition). Boston: Allyn and Bacon.

Bernhardt, E. B. 1991. *Reading Development in a Second Language: Theoretical, Empirical, and Classroom Perspectives.* Norwood, N.J.: Ablex.

Bialystok, E. 1997. "Effects of Bilingualism and Biliteracy on Children's Emerging Concepts of Print," *Developmental Psychology,* Vol. 33, 429–40.

Bodrova, E., and D. E. Paynter. 2000. *Early Literacy: New Issues and New Challenges.* A policy brief of Mid-Continent Research for Education and Learning. Aurora, Colo.: McREL.

Booth, A., and J. F. Dunn. 1996. *Family-School Links: How They Affect Educational Outcomes.* Mahwah, N.J.: Lawrence Erlbaum.

Brassel, D. 2004. "Friday's Authors," *The Journal of Communication and Education,* Vol. 3, No. 7, 15–19.

Bredekamp, S. 2000. *A Commentary on "What Teachers Need to Know About Language."* Washington, D.C.: Center for Applied Linguistics.

Brice, A., and L. I. Rosa-Lugo. 2000. "Code Switching: A Bridge or a Barrier Between Two Languages?" *Multiple Voices for Ethnically Diverse Exceptional Learners,* Vol. 4, No. 1, 1–12.

Brice, A., and C. Roseberry-McKibbin. 2001. "Choice of Languages in Instruction: One Language or Two?" *Teaching Exceptional Children,* Vol. 33, No. 4, 10–15.

Bronfenbrenner, U. 1979. *The Ecology of Human Development.* Cambridge, Mass.: Harvard University Press.

Buriel, R., and T. De Ment. 1997. "Immigration and Sociocultural Change in Mexican, Chinese, and Vietnamese American Families," in *Immigration and Family: Research and Policy on U.S. Immigrants.* Edited by A. Booth, A. C. Crouter, and N. Landale. Mahwah, N.J.: Lawrence Erlbaum.

Buysse, V., and others. 2004. *Addressing the Needs of Latino Children: A National Survey of State Administrators of Early Childhood Programs.* Chapel Hill, N.C.: FPG Child Development Institute.

Byrd, H. B. 2000. "Effective Provision of Educational Services to Latino-American Children with Special Needs and Gifts," *Multiple Voices for Ethnically Diverse Exceptional Learners,* Vol. 4, No. 1, 54–58.

California Department of Education. 1998. *English–Language Arts Content Standards for California Public Schools, Kindergarten Through Grade Twelve.* Sacramento: California Department of Education.

California Department of Education. 2002. *English-Language Development Standards for California Public Schools, Kindergarten Through Grade Twelve.* Sacramento: California Department of Education.

California Department of Education. 2002. *Recommended Literature, Kindergarten Through Grade Twelve.* Sacramento: California Department of Education.

California Department of Education. 2003. "Even-Start Research-based Early Childhood and Parenting Education Professional Development." Sacramento: California Department of Education .

California Department of Education. 2004. "English Learner Students," in *Fact Book 2004: Handbook of Education Information.* Sacramento: California Department of Education. http://www.cde.ca.gov/re/pn/fb/yr04/English.asp

California Department of Education. 2006. *Fact Book 2006: Handbook of Education Information.* Sacramento, California Department of Education.

Candelaria-Greene, J. 1996. "A Paradigm for Bilingual Special Education in the USA: Lessons from Kenya," *The Bilingual Research Journal,* Vol. 20, Nos. 3 and 4, 545–64.

Case, R. 1985. *Intellectual Development: Birth to Adulthood.* Orlando, Fla.: Academic Press.

Cazden, C. 1988. *Classroom Discourse: The Language of Teaching and Learning.* Portsmouth, N.H.: Heinemann.

Cho, G. 2000. "The Role of Heritage Language in Social Interactions and Relationships: Reflections from a Language Minority Group," *The Bilingual Research Journal,* Vol. 24, No. 4, 333–48.

Cook, E.; M. Klein; and A. Tessier. 2004. *Adapting Early Childhood Curricula for Children in Inclusive Settings.* Prepared in collaboration with Stephen E. Daley. Upper Saddle River, N.J.: Pearson Prentice Hall.

Corson, David. 2001. *Language Diversity and Education.* Manwah, N.J.: Lawrence Erlbaum.

Cummins, J. 1981. "The Role of Primary Language Development in Promoting Educational Success for Language Minority Students," in *Schooling and Language Minority Students: A Theoretical Framework.* Los Angeles: Evaluation, Dissemination, and Assessment Center, California State University, pp. 3–49.

Cummins, J. 1984. *Bilingualism and Special Education: Issues in Assessment and Pedagogy.* Clevedon, England: Multilingual Matters.

Cummins, J. 2000. *Language, Power, and Pedagogy: Bilingual Children in the Crossfire.* Clevedon, England: Multilingual Matters.

Cummins, J. 2001. *Negotiating Identities: Education for Empowerment in a Diverse Society* (Second edition). Los Angeles: California Association for Bilingual Education.

Cummins, J., and M. Swain. 1986. *Bilingualism in Education.* New York: Longman.

"Data-informed Decisions About Cultural Diversity." 2002. *The Special Edge Data,* Vol. 15, No. 3, 1–4.

De León, J., and L. McCarty. 1998. "A Study of Effective Instructional Practices by Monolingual English-speaking and Bilingual/Bicultural Teachers in Five Programs Serving Hispanic Preschoolers with Developmental Disabilities," in *Compendium: Writings on Effective Practices for Culturally and Linguistically Diverse Exceptional Learners.* Edited by B. A. Ford. Reston, Va.: The Council for Exceptional Children.

Demmert, W. G. 2001. *Improving the Academic Performance Among Native American Students: A Review of the Research Literature.* Charleston, W.Va.: ERIC Clearinghouse on Rural Education and Small Schools. ED-99-CO-0027.

Diaz Soto, L.; J. L. Smrekar; and D. L. Nekcovei. 1999. *Preserving Home Languages and Opportunities in the Classroom: Challenges and Opportunities.* Directions in Language and Education, No. 13. Washington, D.C.: National Clearinghouse for Bilingual Education.

DiCerbo, P. A. 2000. *Lessons from Research: What Is the Length of Time It Takes Limited English Proficient Students to Acquire English and Succeed in an All-English Classroom?* NCBE Issue Brief No. 5. Washington, D.C.: National Clearinghouse for Bilingual Education.

Dickinson, D., and M. Smith. 2001. "Supporting Language and Literacy Development in the Preschool Classroom," in *Beginning Literacy with Language: Young Children Learning at Home and School.* Edited by D. Dickinson and P. Tabors. Baltimore, Md.: Paul H. Brookes.

Dickinson, D., and P. Tabors. 2001. *Beginning Literacy with Language: Young Children Learning at Home and School.* Baltimore, Md.: Paul H. Brookes.

Duke, N., and V. Purcell-Gates. 2003. "Genres at Home and at School: Bridging the Known to the New," *The Reading Teacher,* Vol. 57, No. 1, 30–37.

Durgunoglu, A. Y.; W. E. Nagy; and B. J. Hancin-Bhatt. 1993. "Cross-Language Transfer of Phonological Awareness," *Journal of Educational Psychology,* Vol. 85, 453–65.

Durgunoglu, A. Y., and B. Öney. 2000. *Literacy Development in Two Languages: Cognitive and Sociocultural Dimensions of Cross-Language Transfer.* From the proceedings of a research symposium on high standards in reading for students from diverse language groups: research, practice, and policy, April 19–20, 2000. Washington, D.C.: U.S. Department of Education, Office of Bilingual Education and Minority Language Affairs.

Durgunoglu, A. Y., and L. Verhoeven. 1998. *Literacy Development in a Multilingual Context: A Cross-Cultural Perspective.* Mahwah, N.J.: Lawrence Erlbaum.

Escamilla, K. 2000. *Bilingual Means Two: Assessment Issues, Early Literacy, and Spanish-Speaking Children.* From the proceedings of a research symposium on high standards in reading for students from diverse language groups: research, practice, and policy, April 19–20, 2000. Washington, D.C.: U.S. Department of Education, Office of Bilingual Education and Minority Language Affairs.

Espinosa, L. M., and M. S. Burns. 2003. "Early Literacy for Young Children and English-Language Learners," in *Teaching 4- to 8-Year-Olds: Literacy, Math, Multiculturalism, and Classroom Community.* Edited by C. Howes. Baltimore, Md.: Paul H. Brookes.

Faltis, C. 1989. "Code-Switching and Bilingual Schooling: An Examination of Jacobson's New Concurrent Approach," *Journal of Multilingual and Multicultural Development,* Vol. 10, No. 2, 117–27.

Fantini, A. 1985. *Language Acquisition of a Bilingual Child: A Sociolinguistic Perspective.* San Diego: College Hill Press.

Faulstitch Orellana, M. 2003. *In Other Words: Learning from Bilingual Kids' Translating and Interpreting Experiences.* Evanston, Ill.: Northwestern University, School of Education and Social Policy.

Fernandez, A. 1992. "Legal Support for Bilingual Education and Language-Appropriate Related Services for Limited English Proficient Students with Disabilities," *Bilingual Research Journal,* Vol. 16, Nos. 3 and 4, 117–40.

Fishman, J., editor. 2001. *Can Threatened Languages Be Saved? Reversing Language Shift Revisited: A 21st Century Perspective.* Clevedon, England: Multilingual Matters.

Gass, S. M., and L. Selinker. 2001. *Second-Language Acquisition: An Introductory Course* (Second edition). Mahwah, N.J.: Lawrence Erlbaum.

Genishi, C. 1981. "Codeswitching in Chicano Six-Year-Olds," in *Latino Language and Communication.* Edited by R. P. Duran. Norwood, N.J.: Ablex.

Genishi, C. 2002. "Young English-Language Learners: Resourceful in the Classroom," *Young Children,* 66–72.

Gerner de Garcia, B. A. 1995a. "Communication and Language Use in Spanish-Speaking Families of Deaf Children," in *Sociolinguistics in Deaf Communities,* Vol. 1. Edited by C. Lucas. Washington, D.C.: Gallaudet Press, pp. 221–52.

Gerner de Garcia, B. A. 1995b. "ESL Applications for Hispanic Deaf Students," *Bilingual Research Journal,* Vol. 19, Nos. 3 and 4, 452–67.

Gersten, R., and S. Baker. 2001. *Practices for English-Language Learners: Promising Themes and Future Directions.* Denver, Colo.: National Institute for Urban School Improvement.

Geva, E., and E. B. Ryan. 1993. "Linguistic and Cognitive Correlates of Academic Skills in First and Second Languages," *Language Learning,* Vol. 43, 5–42.

Goodz, N. 1994. "Interactions Between Parents and Children in Bilingual Families," in *Educating Second-Language Children: The Whole Child, the Whole Curriculum, the Whole Community.* Edited by F. Genesee. New York: Cambridge University Press.

Gottardo, A., and others. 2001. "Factors Related to English Reading Performance in Children with Chinese as a First Language: More Evidence of Cross-Language Transfer of Phonological Processing," *Journal of Educational Psychology,* Vol. 93, 530–42.

Gregory, E., editor. 1997. *One Child, Many Worlds: Early Learning in Multicultural Communities.* New York: Teachers College Press.

Grosjean, F. 1982. *Life with Two Languages: An Introduction to Bilingualism.* Cambridge, Mass.: Harvard University Press.

Gutierrez, K. D., and B. Rogoff. 2003. "Cultural Ways of Learning: Individual Traits or Repertoires of Practice," *Educational Researcher,* Vol. 32, No. 5, 19–25.

Guttierrez-Clellen, V., and Elizabeth Peña. 2001. "Dynamic Assessment of Diverse Children: A Tutorial," *Language, Speech, and Hearing Services in Schools,* Vol. 32, 212–24.

Hakuta, K. 1974. "A Preliminary Report on the Development of Grammatical Morphemes in a Japanese Girl Learning English as a Second Language," *Working Papers in Bilingualism,* Vol. 4, 18–38.

Hakuta, K. 1986. *Mirror of Language: The Debate on Bilingualism.* New York: Basic Books.

Hamayan, E., and R. Perlman. 1990. *Helping Language Minority Students After They Exit from a Bilingual/ESL Program: A Handbook for Teachers.* NCELA Program Information Series, No. 1. http://www.ncela.gwu.edu/ pubs/pigs/pig1.htm

Harding-Esch, E., and P. Riley. 2003. *The Bilingual Family: A Handbook for Parents* (Second edition). Cambridge, England: Cambridge University Press.

Harrison, A., and others. 1990. "Family Ecologies of Ethnic Minority Children," *Child Development,* Vol. 61, 347–62.

Harry, B. 1992. *Cultural Diversity, Families, and the Special Education System: Communication and Empowerment.* New York: Teachers College Press.

Hart, R. 1979. *Children's Experience of Place.* New York: Irvington.

Hart, B., and T. Risley. 1995. *Meaningful Differences in the Everyday Experience of Young American Children.* Baltimore, Md.: Paul H. Brookes.

Heath, S. B. 1983. *Ways with Words: Language, Life, and Work in Communities and Classrooms.* New York: Cambridge University Press.

Hirsh-Pasek, K.; A. Kochanoff; and N. Newcombe. 2005. "Using Scientific Knowledge to Inform Preschool Assessment: Making the Case for 'Empirical Validity,' " *Social Policy Report,* Vol. 19, No. 1, 3–19.

Igoa, I. 1995. *The Inner World of the Immigrant Child.* Mahwah, N.J.: Lawrence Erlbaum.

Individuals with Disabilities Education Act Amendments of 1997. Public Law No. 94–142, 89 Stat. 773 (as amended), renamed IDEA, Public Law No. 101-476, 104 Stat. 1143 (codified as amended at 20 U.S.C. x 1400 et seq.) (1994), amended by the IDEA Amendments of 1997, Public Law No. 105–17.

Individuals with Disabilities Education Act. 1997. Final Regulations, Assistance to States for the Education of Children with Disabilities, 34 C.F.R., Part 300 (March 12, 1999). http://www.ed.gov/offices/osers/policy/idea/regs.html

International Reading Association. 1998. "Learning to Read and Write: Developmentally Appropriate Practices for Young Children: A joint position statement of the International Reading Association (IRA) and the National Association for the Education of Young Children (NAEYC)," *The Reading Teacher,* Vol. 52, No. 2, 193–216.

International Reading Association. 1999. *Using Multiple Methods of Beginning Reading Instruction: A Position Statement of the International Reading Association.* Newark, Del.: International Reading Association.

Irujo, S. 1986. "Don't Put Your Leg in Your Mouth: Transfer in the Acquisition of Idioms in Second Language," *TESOL Quarterly,* Vol. 20, 287–304.

Isbell, R. 2002. "Learning Language and Literacy: Telling and Retelling Stories," *Young Children,* Vol. 57, No. 2, 26–30.

Jacobsen, R. 1990. *Codeswitching as a Worldwide Phenomenon.* New York; P. Lang.

Jiménez, R., and R. B. Barrera. 2001. "How Will Bilingual/ESL Programs in Literacy Change in the Next Millennium?" *Reading Research Quarterly,* Vol. 36, 522–23.

Jiménez, R.; G. E. García; and D. Pearson. 1995. "Three Children, Two Languages, and Strategic Reading: Case Studies in Bilingual/Monolingual Reading," *American Education Research Journal,* Vol. 32, 31–61.

Kaderavek, J. N., and L. Justice. 2004. "Embedded, Explicit, Emergent Literacy Intervention II: Goal Selection and Implementation in the Early Childhood Classroom," *Language, Speech, and Hearing Services in Schools,* Vol. 35, 212–28.

Kasper, G., and K. Rose. 2003. *Pragmatic Development in a Second Language.* Malden, Mass.: Blackwell.

Klinger, J., and A. Artiles. 2003. "When Should Bilingual Students Be in Special Education?" *Educational Leadership,* Vol. 61, No. 2, 66–71.

Koralek, D., and R. Collins. 1997. *On the Road to Reading: A Guide for Community Partners.* Vienna, Va.: The Early Childhood Technical Assistance Center. Available at 1-800-616-2242.

Lambert, W. E. 1978. "Cognitive and Socio-Cultural Consequences of Bilingualism," *Canadian Modern Language Review,* Vol. 34, 537–47.

Lanauze, M., and C. E. Snow. 1989. "The Relation Between First- and Second-Language Skills: Evidence from Puerto Rican Elementary School Children in Bilingual Programs," *Linguistics and Education,* Vol. 1, 323–40.

Lee, P. 1996. "Cognitive Development in Bilingual Children: A Case for Bilingual Instruction in Early Childhood Education," *The Bilingual Research Journal,* Vol. 20, Nos. 3–4, 499–522.

Legislative Analyst's Office. 2004. "A Look at the Progress of English Learner Students: Executive Summary." http://www.lao.ca.gov/2004/english_learners/021204_english_learners.htm

Leopold, W. F. 1949. *Speech Development of a Bilingual Child: A Linguist's Record.* In four volumes. (Vol. 1: *Vocabulary Growth in the First Two Years.* Vol. 2: *Sound Learning in the First Two Years.* Vol. 3: *Grammar and General Problems in the First Two Years.* Vol. 4: *Diary from Age Two*). Evanston, Ill.: Northwestern University Press.

LoCastro, V. B. 2003. *An Introduction to Pragmatics: Social Action for Language Teachers.* Ann Arbor: University of Michigan Press.

Lopez, E. S., and P. L. de Cos. 2004. *Preschool and Childcare Enrollment in California.* Sacramento: California Research Bureau.

Marcos, K. 1999. *Are We Wasting Our Nation's Language Resources? Heritage Languages in America.* ERIC/CLL Language Link. http://www.cal.org/ericcll/langlink/1099.html (accessed 12-29-05)

McClure, E. 1977. "Aspects of Code-switching in the Discourse of Bilingual Mexican-American Children," in *Linguistics and Anthropology.* Edited by M. Saviile-Troike. Washington, D.C.: Georgetown University School of Languages and Linguistics.

McDaniel, K. 2002. "Who Needs Special Education? Addressing the Issue of Disproportionate Representation," *The Special Edge Data,* Vol. 15, No. 2, 3–4.

McLaughlin, B. 1984. *Second-Language Acquisition in Childhood.* Volume 1, *Preschool Children* (Second edition). Hillsdale, N.J.: Lawrence Erlbaum.

McLaughlin, B., and B. McLeod. 1996. *Educating All Our Students: Improving Education for Children from Culturally and Linguistically Diverse Backgrounds.* Final report of the National Center for Research on Cultural Diversity and Second Language.

Miles, C. 1996. "Bilingual Children in Special Education: Acquisition of Language and Culture by British Pakistani Children Attending a School for Pupils with Severe Learning Difficulties." Unpublished thesis, University of Birmingham, England.

Moats, L. C. 2000. *Speech to Print: Language Essentials for Teachers.* Baltimore, Md.: Paul H. Brookes.

Mohanty, A. K. 1990. "Psychological Consequences of Mother-Tongue Maintenance and the Language of Literacy for Linguistic Minorities in India," *Psychology and Developing Societies,* Vol. 2, 31–51.

Mundy, P., and others. 1995. "Nonverbal Communication and Early Language Acquisition in Children with Down Syndrome and in Normal Developing Children," *Journal of Speech, Language and Hearing Research,* Vol. 38, 157–67.

Natheson-Mejía, and K. Escamilla. 2003. "Connecting with Latino Children: Bridging Cultural Gaps with Children's Literature," *Bilingual Research Journal,* Vol. 27, No. 1, 101–16.

National Association for the Education of Young Children (NAEYC). 1996. *Responding to Linguistic and Cultural Diversity: Recommendations for Effective Early Childhood Education.* An NAEYC position statement. Washington, D.C.: National Association for the Education of Young Children.

National Institute on Child Health and Human Development. 2000. *Teaching Children to Read: An Evidence-based Assessment of the Scientific Research Literature on Reading and Its Implications for Reading Instruction.* Developed by the National Reading Panel. Washington, D.C.: National Institute on Child Health and Human Development.

Neuman, S. B.; C. Copple; and S. Bredekamp. 2000. *Learning to Read and Write: Developmentally Appropriate Practices for Young Children.* Washington, D.C.: National Association for the Education of Young Children.

Ochs, E., and B. Schieffelin. 1984. "Language Acquisition and Socialization: Three Developmental Stories and Their Implications," in *Culture Theory: Essays on Mind, Self, and Emotion.* Edited by R. Shweder and R. LeVine. Cambridge, England: Cambridge University Press, pp. 276–320.

Ortiz, A. A., and E. Maldonado-Colon. 1986. "Recognizing Learning Disabilities in Bilingual Children: How to Lessen Inappropriate Referrals to Special Education," *Journal of Reading, Writing, and Learning Disabilities International,* Vol. 2, No. 1, 43–47.

Ovando, C., and V. Collier. 1998. *Bilingual and ESL Classrooms: Teaching in Multicultural Contexts* (Second edition). Boston: McGraw Hill.

Owocki, G. 2001. *Make Way for Literacy: Teaching the Way Young Children Learn.* Washington, D.C.: National Association for the Education of Young Children.

Oxford, R. 1982. "Research on Language Loss: A Review of Implications for Foreign Language Teaching," *Modern Language Journal,* Vol. 66, 160–69.

Palincsar, A. S., and L. Klenk. 1992. "Fostering Literacy Learning in Supportive Contexts," *Journal of Learning Disabilities,* Vol. 25, No. 4, 211–25.

Pease-Alvarez, L. 1993. *Moving In and Out of Bilingualism: Investigating Native Language Maintenance and Shift in Mexican-Descent Children.* Santa Cruz, Calif.: National Center for Research on Cultural Diversity and Second Language Learning.

Pérez, B., editor. 2004. *Sociocultural Contexts of Language and Literacy* (Second edition). Mahwah, N.J.: Lawrence Erlbaum.

Pérez, B., and M. E. Torres-Guzmán. 1996. *Learning in Two Worlds: An Integrated Spanish/English Biliteracy Approach.* White Plains, N.Y.: Longman.

Peynircioglu, Z. F., and A. Y. Durgunoglu. 1993. "When Bilingual Presentation Helps Memory: Effects of Bilingual Context on Memory Performance," in *Cognition and Culture: A Cross-Cultural Approach to Psychology.* Edited by J. Altarriba. Amsterdam: Elsevier Science Publishers, pp. 57–75.

Peynircioglu, Z. F., and A. Tekcan. 1993. "Word Perception in Two Languages," *Journal of Memory and Language,* Vol. 32, 390–401.

Pinnegar, S.; A. Teemant; and S. Tyra. 2001. *The Early Childhood Literacy Case: A Video Ethnography of Balanced Literacy Approaches for Second-Language Students.* Washington, D.C.: Center for Applied Linguistics.

Pransky, K., and F. Bailey. 2003. "To Meet Your Students Where They Are, First You Have to Find Them: Working with Culturally and Linguistically Diverse At-Risk Students," *The Reading Teacher,* Vol. 56, No. 4, 370–83.

Ramirez, J. D. 2000. *Bilingualism and Literacy: Problem or Opportunity? A Synthesis of Reading Research on Bilingual Students.* From the proceedings of a research symposium on high standards in reading for students from diverse language groups: research, practice, and policy, April 19–20, 2000. Washington, D.C.: U.S. Department of Education, Office of Bilingual Education and Minority Language Affairs.

Reading Rockets. 2004. A national multimedia project that looks at how young children learn to read, why so many struggle, and how caring adults can help. Includes printed guides for viewers, educators, and families; a comprehensive Web site at http://www.readingrockets.org; and a Web site for Spanish-speaking parents at http://www.colorincolorado.org.

Richman, L. 2003. "Special Education: Integrating Language Disorder and Social Perception," *The Journal of Communication and Education,* Vol. 3, No. 4.

Roache, M., and others. 2003. "An Investigation of Collaboration Among School Professionals in Serving Culturally and Linguistically Diverse Students with Exceptionalities," *Bilingual Research Journal,* Vol. 27, No. 1, 117–36.

Romero, M., and A. Parrino. 1994. "Planned Alternation of Languages (PAL): Language Use and Distribution in Bilingual Classrooms," *The Journal of Educational Issues of Language Minority Students,* Vol. 13, 137–61.

Ruiz, N.; E. Vargas; and A. Beltran. 2002. "Becoming a Reader and a Writer in a Bilingual Special Education Classroom," *Language Arts,* Vol. 79, No. 4, 297–309.

Saville-Troike, M. 1989. *The Ethnography of Communication: An Introduction* (Second edition). Cambridge, Mass.: Blackwell.

Scarcella, R. 1990. *Teaching Language Minority Students in the Multicultural Classroom.* Englewood Cliffs, N.J.: Prentice Hall.

Schieffelin, B. 1979. "How Kaluli Children Learn What to Say, What to Do, and How to Feel: An Ethnographic Study of the Development of Communicative Competence." New York: Columbia University (doctoral dissertation).

Schinke-Llano, L., and R. Rauff, editors. 1996. *New Ways in Teaching Young Children.* Alexandria, Va.: Teachers of English to Speakers of Other Languages, Inc.

Schon, I. 1997. *The Best of Latino Heritage: A Guide to the Best Juvenile Books About Latino People and Cultures.* Landham, Md.: Scarecrow Press.

Serrano, R., and E. Howard. 2003. *Maintaining Spanish Proficiency in the United States: The Influence of English on the Spanish Writing of Native Spanish Speakers in Two-Way Immersion Programs.* Santa Cruz, Calif.: Center for Research on Education, Diversity, and Excellence.

Shanahan, T., and D. Strickland. 2004. "Laying the Groundwork for Literacy: The National Early Literacy Panel Synthesis of Research on Early Literacy Education." *Educational Leadership,* Vol. 61, No. 2.

Shefelbine, J. 1998. "Academic Language and Literacy Development." Paper presented at the Reading and English-Language Learner Forum, Reading Literature Project, Sacramento, California.

Shonkoff, J. P., and D. A. Phillips, editors. 2000. *From Neurons to Neighborhoods. The Science of Early Childhood Development.* Washington, D.C.: National Academy Press.

Slavin, R., and A. Cheung. 2003. *Effective Reading Programs for English Language Learners: A Best-Evidence Synthesis.* Baltimore, Md.: Johns Hopkins University.

Snow, C.; S. Burns; and P. Griffin. 1998. *Preventing Reading Difficulties.* Washington, D.C.: National Research Council.

Strickland, D. S., and others. 2004. "Distinguished Educator: The Role of Literacy in Early Childhood Education," *The Reading Teacher,* Vol. 58, No. 1, 86–100.

Suarez-Orozco, M., and C. Suarez-Orozco. 2001. *Children of Immigration.* Cambridge, Mass.: Harvard University Press.

Tabors, P. 1997. *One Child, Two Languages.* Baltimore, Md.: Paul H. Brookes.

Tabors, P. 1998. "What Early Childhood Educators Need to Know: Developing Effective Programs for Linguistically and Culturally Diverse Children and Families," *Young Children,* Vol. 53, No. 6, 20–26.

Tabors, P.; M. Paez; and L. Lopez. 2003. "Dual Language Abilities of Bilingual Four-Year-Olds: Initial Findings from the Early Childhood Study of Language and Literacy Development of Spanish-Speaking Children," *NABE Journal of Research and Practice,* Vol. 1, No. 1, 70–91.

Tabors, P., and C. Snow. 1994. "English as a Second Language in Preschool Programs," in *Educating Second Language Children: The Whole Child, the Whole Curriculum, the Whole Community.* Edited by F. Genesse. New York: Cambridge University Press.

Tabors, P., and C. Snow. 2001. "Young Bilingual Children and Early Literacy Development," in *Handbook of Early Literacy Research.* Edited by S. Neuman and D. Dickinson. New York: Guilford Press.

Tafoya, S. 2002. "The Linguistic Landscape of California Schools," *California Counts,* Vol. 3, No. 4.

TESOL. 1997. *TESOL ESL Standards for Pre-K–12 Students*. Alexandria, Va.: Teachers of English to Speakers of Other Languages (TESOL), Inc.

TESOL. 2001. *TESOL Statement on Language and Literacy Development for Young English Language Learners: Advancing the Profession*. http://www.tesol.org/assoc/statement/2001-youngells.html

Thomas, W., and V. Collier. 1997. *School Effectiveness for Language Minority Students*. NCBE Resource Collection Series, No. 9. Washington, D.C.: National Clearinghouse for Bilingual Education.

Thomas, W., and V. Collier. 2002. *A National Study of School Effectiveness for Language Minority Students' Long-Term Academic Achievement*. Santa Cruz: University of California, Santa Cruz, Center for Research on Education, Diversity, and Excellence.

Thomas, W., and V. Collier. 2003a. "The Multiple Benefits of Dual Language," *Educational Leadership*, Vol. 61, No. 2, 61–65.

Thomas, W., and V. Collier. 2003b. *What We Know About Effective Instructional Approaches for Language Minority Learners*. Arlington, Va.: Educational Research Service.

Tompkins, M. 2002. "Sign with Your Baby: Opening the Doors to Communication," *Infant Development Association of California News*, Vol. 29, No. 1.

Torgesen, J. K. 2002. "The Prevention of Reading Difficulties," *Journal of School Psychology*, Vol. 40, No. 1, 7–26.

Torgeson, J. K., and P. Matheson. 2001. "What Every Teacher Should Know About Phonological Awareness," in *The CORE Reading Research Anthology: The Why of Reading Instruction*. Novato, Calif.: Arena Press, pp. 38–46.

Tucker, G. R. 1999. *A Global Perspective on Bilingualism and Bilingual Education*. Center for Applied Linguistics Digest. EDO-FL-99-04. http://cal.org/resources/digest/author.html#t

U.S. Bureau of the Census. 2003. *Language Use and English-speaking Ability: Census 2000 Brief*. Report No. C2K3R-29. Washington, D.C. U. S. Bureau of the Census. http://www.census.gov/population/www/cen2000/phc-tao.html

U.S. Bureau of the Census. 2004. http://www.census.gov

U. S. Department of Education. 2002. *Helping Your Child Become a Reader* (Second edition). Telephone: 1-877-433-7827 or 1-800-437-0833 (for TTD or TTY); or at http://www.ed.gov/parents/academic/help/reader/index.html.

Valdés, G. 1996. *Con respeto. Bridging the Differences Between Culturally Diverse Families and Schools*. New York: Teachers College.

Valdés, G. 2003. *Expanding Definitions of Giftedness: The Case of Young Interpreters from Immigrant Communities*. Mahwah, N.J.: Lawrence Erlbaum.

Vasquez, O. A.; L. Pease-Alvarez; and S. M.Shannon. 1994. *Pushing Boundaries: Language and Culture in a Mexicano Community.* New York: Cambridge University Press.

Wagner, D. A.; J. E. Spratt; and A. Ezzaki. 1989. "Does Learning to Read in a Second Language Always Put the Child at a Disadvantage? Some Counter Evidence from Morocco," *Applied Psycholinguistics,* Vol. 10, 31–48.

Wald, J. 1996. *Culturally and Linguistically Diverse Professionals in Special Education: A Demographic Analysis.* Reston, Va.: Council for Exceptional Children.

Wilkinson, C. Y., and A. A. Ortiz. 1986. *Characteristics of Limited English Proficient and English Proficient Learning Disabled Hispanic Students at Initial Assessment and at Reevaluation.* Austin: University of Texas, Department of Special Education, Handicapped Minority Research Institute on Language Proficiency. ERIC Document Reproduction Service No. ED 283 314.

Winsler, A., and others. 1999. "When Learning a Second Language Does Not Mean Losing the First: Bilingual Language Development in Low-Income Spanish-speaking Children Attending Bilingual Preschool," *Child Development,* Vol. 70, No. 2, 349–62.

Wong Fillmore, L. 1990. "Language and Cultural Issues in the Early Education of Language Minority Children," in *The Care and Education of America's Young Children: Obstacles and Opportunities.* Edited by S. L. Kagan. Chicago: University of Chicago Press.

Wong Fillmore, L. 1991. "When Learning a Second Language Means Losing the First," *Early Childhood Research Quarterly,* Vol. 6, No. 3, 323–47.

Wong Fillmore, L., and C. Snow. 2000. *What Teachers Need to Know About Language.* Washington, D.C.: Center for Applied Linguistics.

Yeung, A. S.; H. W. Marsh; and R. Suliman. 2000. "Can Two Languages Live in Harmony?" Analysis of the National Education Longitudinal Study of 1988 (NELS88) Longitudinal Data on Maintenance of Home Language, *American Educational Research Journal,* Vol. 37, 1001–26.

Zentella, A. C. 1997. *Growing Up Bilingual.* Malden, Mass.: Blackwell.

05-013 PD061005-656 1-07 20M